CONFERENCE PROCEEDINGS

RAND

The RAND Forum on Cuba

Edited by Edward Gonzalez and Richard A. Nuccio

National Security Research Division

PREFACE

With funding provided by The Ford Foundation, RAND organized and convened "The RAND Forum on Cuba," which was held in three sessions in Washington, D.C., on February 19-20, April 16-17, and May 28-29, 1998. The Forum provided a non-partisan venue for a diverse group of individuals from in and outside the U.S. Government to discuss, according to a structured, interactive format, where Cuba is headed over the short- to medium-term, why Cuba is important to U.S. interests, and what should U.S. policy be toward a Cuba under and after Castro.

This report reprints the Summaries of each of those interactive sessions, along with the list of discussion questions that preceded each session. It includes a concluding essay co-authored by the Forum's Organizer and Advisor that analyzes both the Forum's recommendations and more recent U.S. policy initiatives.

The Forum was part of a long-standing and continuing RAND research program on Cuba and other communist states. The Forum was convened under the auspices of the International Security and Defense Policy Center of RAND's National Security Research Division (NSRD), which conducts research for the U.S. Department of Defense, for other U.S. government agencies, and for other institutions.

v

ACKNOWLEDGMENTS

The Forum organizers wish to thank Ms. Cristina Eguizábal of
The Ford Foundation for her wise counsel and participation in the
Forum, as well as The Ford Foundation itself for the grant that
made the Forum possible. The Forum organizers also wish to extend
their profound appreciation to all the participants, lead
discussants, and commentators, for their incisive insights,
constructive discourse, and much appreciated civility throughout
all three Forum sessions. Finally, a word of gratitude is in
order for Rosalie Heacock for shouldering a heavy secretarial load
under often hectic, trying circumstances prior to each of the
Forum sessions, and for doing so with care, grace and goodwill.

CONTENTS

I. INTRODUCTION

In February, April, and May 1998, members of the policy community gathered together to participate in "The RAND Forum on Cuba." The participants consisted of Congressional staff members, State Department and NSC officials, members of the intelligence community, former Ambassadors and other former government officials, non-government foreign policy generalists, academic specialists on Cuba, and representatives of non-governmental organizations dealing with Cuba. The purpose of the Forum was to: (1) increase the awareness of participants concerning recent Cuban developments and trends; (2) convince generalists in particular that Cuba is a serious foreign--and not just a domestic--policy problem for the United States; and (3) advance the policy debate over Cuba and, if possible, work toward a policy consensus among the participants.

The Forum was held in three one and one-half day sessions in Washington, D.C.. Guided by a Moderator, each of the sessions was interactive whereby some thirty-five to forty participants were asked to discuss the Cuba issue according to three separate but related areas based on an agenda and list of questions. In the first session, held February 19-20, participants examined developments and trends in present-day Cuba. In the second, held April 16-17, they focused on U.S. interests in Cuba and the effect on those interests of different transition outcomes in a post-Castro Cuba. In the last session, on May 28-29, the participants assessed current U.S. policy and different policy alternatives.

The Forum's first and second sessions started off with academic specialists who served as "Lead Discussants" to help frame the issues, with representatives of NGOs and policy organizations performing that function in the May session. All sessions had two "Commentators" who synthesized the previous day's deliberations and findings, and made their own observations.

Summaries of the first and second sessions were distributed to participants prior to the next session in order to provide a degree of continuity from one session to the next. These Summaries, along the Summary of the third and last session, are reprinted in this report in their original form.

The Forum organizers had no predetermined policy outcome as their aim. Instead, the Forum's findings and recommendations-- which are reflected in the Summaries of the sessions that follow-- were the result of searching, probing discussions among all the participants over sometimes contentious policy questions. The give-and-take among some thirty-five or forty participants was seldom tidy, but it was generally civil and certainly productive. Surprisingly, as revealed by the Summaries, the participants came to a far greater degree of agreement than had been originally anticipated, even on the most contentious issue--the U.S. embargo, the Helms-Burton Law, and the alternatives to present policy. Hence, the Forum constituted a modest but welcomed step in moving the policy debate forward. Rather than remaining mired in sterile debate, it created the kind of atmosphere needed for the Executive Branch, Congress, and the attentive public to begin finding a greater degree of common ground on Cuba.

In January 1999, the Administration announced several new initiatives in its Cuba policy based on the recommendations of a Task Force of the Council on Foreign Relations, which paralleled some of the earlier recommendations and conclusions made by the Forum. The new policy initiatives, the reaction to them, and the Forum's own conclusions, are all analyzed in a special essay on the "The Cuban Conundrum" that follows the Summary of the May session.

II. SESSION I: CUBA TODAY AND PROSPECTS FOR PEACEFUL OR VIOLENT CHANGE

Session I of The RAND Forum on Cuba:

Cuba Today and Prospects for Peaceful or Violent Change

by
Phyllis Greene Walker, Forum Rapporteur
and
Edward Gonzalez, Forum Organizer

On February 19-20, 1998, the first session of a three-part RAND forum on Cuba was convened. The aim of this first session was to consider the present situation on the island and evaluate the prospects for change. The remaining two sessions, to be held in April and May, will address U.S. interests and stakes in Cuban transition outcomes and U.S. policy options, respectively. This off-the-record session, which was held over a day-and-a-half, was attended by some thirty-five individuals. Participants included present and former policymakers, congressional aides and committee staff, intelligence analysts, academic and other specialists, and two foreign diplomats.

Summary

Cuba continues to be gripped by many of the same forces of political decay and economic deterioration that affected Eastern Europe and the former Soviet Union. As a result, the state has been seriously weakened to the extent that Castro's Cuba has entered a post-totalitarian phase like its former communist brethren. It thus cannot fully control society nearly as much as in the past. However, unless major unforeseen developments were to arise, a regime transition toward a market economy and democratic polity does not appear likely in the near future, whether under Castro or after Castro.

The Castro regime has thus far muddled through its present crisis by successfully improvising within constricted parameters:

• The economy severely contracted following the disappearance of the Soviet Union, but foreign investments and tourism have partially compensated for the loss of Soviet largesse;

• The pressures for political change continue to build, but remain manageable due to state repression and an atomized opposition;

• The prevalence of corruption in both state and society has become endemic, but this also helps lessen social tensions;

• The regime has become divided over the question of reform, but internal cohesion still remains relatively strong because all its members have a stake in its long-term survival;

• The military has lost much of its traditional mission, but it has been redirected into new economic pursuits and shows little sign of disloyalty or anti-regime sentiment; and

• The leadership is old and ailing, but the regime is making preparations for a "managed succession."

While prospects for a violent transition have now been reduced, a new economic contraction would most surely intensify social tensions on the island. This could oblige the Castro leadership to enact further limited economic reforms of the type that it promulgated prior to 1995--or to use greater repression in order to stay in power as it has done in recent years. At present, political dissent continues to manifest itself, but it has not been transformed into a broad opposition movement owing in part to the effectiveness of the state's security apparatus. Still, the state has had to loosen its grip over the populace and the Pope's visit in January may accelerate the rebuilding and strengthening of civil society. However, this process could take years.

A governmental succession--as distinct from regime transition--might well take place within the not too distant future due to Fidel Castro's worsening state of health. The regime's vulnerability to both internal and external pressures for change is certain to be most acute following his demise, especially were it to coincide with a new economic crisis. Nevertheless, if the leadership is successful in its present efforts to manage the succession process, his departure may not necessarily produce fundamental system change. If the new team is composed of Raúl Castro, Ricardo Alarcón, and others drawn from the present leadership, the new government will remain essentially Leninist. At best, it may enact more liberalizing reforms for the economy but not the polity as it seeks to assert its control over a Cuba without Fidel.

I. Cuba's Transition Toward Post-Totalitarianism

The general consensus among participants was that the Castro regime is undergoing a slow process of political decay set in motion by the collapse of the Soviet Union and the economic crisis that ensued after 1991. As a consequence, Cuba is being transformed from a totalitarian to a post-totalitarian or authoritarian state that is less driven by ideology, less capable of mobilizing the populace, and less in control of all aspects of Cuban life. Even though it is still strong, the tight grip of the state has thus begun to loosen over society.

With the contraction of the state-run economy, Cubans are no longer heavily dependent upon the state. Members of the armed forces and government as well as the general population must resort to the black market, legal and illegal self-employment, and other illicit activities --including prostitution--to survive. As government control has weakened, works by banned authors are now available on the black market. Despite suffering banishment and

repression, human rights and dissident groups repeatedly reemerge
in newly reconstituted groups.

II. Economic Crisis and Limited Reforms

Faced with an acute economic crisis, the regime's
strategy for survival in a post-communist world has rested upon a
mixture of limited reforms and state repression. On the economic
front, it has demonstrated just enough economic pragmatism
regarding foreign investments and tourism to enable it to muddle
through the crisis. As one participant pointed out, Fidel Castro
has been obliged to do things he doesn't want, and publicly at
least to deplore the course of action that he has been forced to
adopt, because the courting of foreign investments and tourism,
and the dollarization of the economy, go against the very precepts
of his ultra-nationalistic revolution.

Although the regime's strategy for survival has succeeded
thus far, the economic crisis has not subsided all that much.
Food and most other basic commodity shortages remain acute, and
Cubans must rely on their own ingenuity and devices, and various
illicit activities for their economic survival. One participant
observed that, contrary to what he had expected prior to his visit
to the island, conditions in the countryside were worse than in
Havana and other major cities.

It was noted that the government has had to juggle three
conflictive goals in its strategy for survival--the new quest for
greater economic efficiency, the preservation of a social safety
net, and the maintenance of political control. The push for
economic efficiency in the early 1990s not only conflicted with
the population's expectations concerning continued socio-economic
entitlements, but also began undermining the state's control over
society. As a consequence, the regime not only significantly
slowed the pace of economic reforms by the end of 1994, but also
soon after began a political crackdown. The repression of
dissidents, human rights activists, and others outside the regime
intensified through 1996 and into 1997. The crackdown also
targeted reformers within the regime, as some were removed from
research institutes or otherwise silenced during the first half of
1996.

Despite the fact that economic reforms have been stalled
over the past three years, some participants believe that the
pendulum could swing back. For the second year in a row, a poor
sugar harvest is expected for 1998. Together with official
government reports that the economy will continue to grow at only
slightly over two percent per annum, this development could
strengthen the hand of reformers. Meanwhile, somewhat greater
intellectual freedom is currently being tolerated, as reflected by
the ability of some think tanks to pursue quietly their studies on
reforms for possible future implementation. If the economy stalls
and popular unrest grows, then Castro and other hardliners could
be obliged to again permit new liberalizing reforms.

Were further reforms to be implemented, however, they
may well be bounded by the popular consensus concerning the

proyecto social (social project), which entails the belief that all Cubans are entitled to employment, national health care, education, and other social goods. The leadership is well aware that its commitment to these social goals provides it with a measure of its popular legitimacy--a legitimacy that would be eroded by policies of economic liberalization that adversely affect such traditional political constituencies as party cadres. government workers, pensioners, and other fixed-salaried sectors the populace who receive their income in *pesos*. This concern in turn is used against the economic policy recommendations of the reformers. In this same vein, the possible loss of social goods under a liberal democratic government was thought to inhibit broader popular support for fundamental system change--a fear that the regime constantly exploits.

III. Stasis on the Political Front

The participants found no reason to believe that any political reforms could be expected under the current leadership. Despite signs of a "loosened grip" by Cuba's post-totalitarian state, the regime retains a formidable repressive apparatus which it employs to control dissent and destroy any signs of organized opposition. Moreover, a slight loosening or tolerance by the government concerning personal behavior may be used as an escape valve that helps the regime maintain societal control. Even the growing prevalence of corruption in and outside the government helps to facilitate the maintenance of political control by the regime.

With the government's decision to open the island to foreign investments, the top leadership evidently reached a consensus regarding the necessity for Cuba's reintegration into what has now become a post-communist world. But this reintegration has its limits: it is deemed acceptable only if it does not involve high political costs for the regime nor adversely affect the core values and interests upon which the regime is based. Thus, several participants pointed out, Fidel Castro rejected the European Union's efforts to broker a deal between Cuba and the United States in early 1996 because, among other things, it would have required his government to decriminalize political dissent and accept dissident or opposition groups like *Concilio Cubano*.

As the leadership strives to survive in the new international environment, participants noted that the Cuban people are more concerned with daily economic survival than with larger political issues. While this "fleeing of politics" withdraws active support from Castro and the government, and constrains the latter's ability to mobilize the population, it also serves to reduce the likelihood for the development of serious domestic political opposition. This trend toward apolitical behavior may mean that Cubans place a high value on political stability even though they may want more political space as was indicated by the cries for "*libertad*" that were frequently heard during the papal masses in January.

It was pointed out that the leadership is aware of the weakening in the belief system that has helped undergird the revolution and the regime. The Fifth Congress of the Communist Party of Cuba (PCC), held in October 1997, sought to address this problem by trying to revitalize the PCC. The Party is seeking to attract youth, who, as one participant found when he visited Cuba, generally tend to be less supportive of the Revolution than their parents. Several young provincial leaders were thus appointed to the Politburo. Party stalwarts were also elected to the Central Committee, in contrast to previous PCC congresses where Central Committee membership was often given as a reward for good performance in areas of activities outside the Party.

One participant observed that a careful distinction should be made between the popular disregard for the Party as an institution and the respect often accorded to individual PCC members, particularly at the local level. It was noted that there has been an increase in the strength of local party forces, who often embrace a more populist style of politics at the grassroots level. Like their fellow citizens, local party cadres tend to be more concerned with seeing that the buses run than with larger political issues--a trend that could have an effect on politics within the PCC as well as on the Party's role in both a Cuba under and after Castro.

IV. State and Society

As was noted earlier, one significant trend in Cuba's post-totalitarian transition has been the "loosening" of the state's grip over society. Another accompanying trend has been the rise in endemic corruption in the government and population at large. Over time, both could erode the regime's ability to maintain its authority and control over society.

The first trend is evident in the continuing "renewal of political dissent." Even though the state's repressive capabilities have not diminished, new groups continually reemerge to replace those that have been forcibly disbanded; and new people step forward to replace those dissidents who have been jailed or exiled, and to denounce the regime. Although far from constituting an opposition political movement, they stand--in the words of one participant--as brave "witnesses" to Cuba's present travail.

So far, the government has decided not to forcefully quash all opposition. One reason for this is that Cuba's dissidents are still very much fragmented and constitute "political atoms," as one participant described them. At present, they pose more of an irritation to the regime than a serious threat. Nonetheless, should the dissidents become better organized or gain wider popular support, the government would most certainly would move against them in a more decisive fashion, even though such heavy-handed repression would incur high domestic and international costs for the regime.

The significance of Pope John Paul II's visit last January was assessed within this political context. Many participants thought the pontiff's agenda in Cuba was to use the Church to open political space so that civil society might become stronger, much as occurred after his visit to Poland. The phrase, "do not be afraid," was thus often repeated during his three masses. On the other hand, unlike the Church in Poland, some participants pointed out the Catholic Church in Cuba has always been relatively weak to the extent that its ability to 'empower' civil society may be limited. In interpreting the Church's interests in Cuba, some saw more a "religious entrepreneurial" objective in the visit in terms of countering the growing influence and support for Afro-Cuban and Pentecostal religions.

The second trend, which is sure to have adverse long-term implications for the future of a democratic Cuba, was the spread of the black market and, along with it, what might be described as the routinization of corruption and law-breaking behavior among the populace. Cubans have long had to engage in "gray behavior" that bordered on illegality in order to survive. But several participants considered it significant that outright illegal behavior is becoming endemic among the general populace, and that it now includes government officials who are stealing or taking bribes.

However, others saw a parallel between the Cuban government's apparent toleration of "gray behavior" and the situation that existed in pre-1989 Eastern Europe and in the Soviet Union under Brezhnev: tolerating such behavior served to aid government control, with the black market and illicit activities providing a "release valve" for social tensions that might otherwise explode. In any event, the disregard for legality is a troubling development and bodes ill for Cuba's future, particularly in light of the prevalence of widespread corruption in Cuba's pre-revolutionary past, including organized crime during the Batista era.

V. Regime Stability and Continuity

Participants addressed the issue as to whether a continuation of the present difficult economic situation or an unforeseen development was likely to affect regime stability and continuity. The discussion focused on the implications for the regime were Cuba to continue to experience poor economic performance, which was defined as annual gross domestic product failing to grow more quickly than at the present rate of just over two percent. One participant argued that, given the poor prospects for Cuba's economic future, the continuing failure to achieve quicker economic growth might either lead to social unrest or oblige the regime to carry out, albeit unwillingly, more extensive economic reforms.

Other participants were not so sure. Given Cuba's low birth rate, they argued that an annual growth rate of 2 to 3 percent was probably adequate to ensure continuing stability, and that a prediction of social chaos, or even regime failure, was unwarranted. Notwithstanding this, it was considered possible that an unforeseen crisis, such as a natural disaster, could throw off the trend line. As one participant noted, however, even though we cannot dismiss the possibility of unexpected change, neither can we anticipate it.

9

Some participants raised the issue as to whether the regime itself might choose to provoke a crisis, possibly in order to relieve pressures for change. This could include a peaceful "invasion" of Guantanamo by unarmed civilians marching on the base in a nonviolent demonstration or even a government-encouraged mass exodus of disgruntled Cubans from the island. Some questioned whether Fidel Castro might secretly desire a U.S. invasion, and that he might provoke one were he to conclude that his regime's failure was inevitable and that, as a consequence, his historical legacy was at risk. Similarly, U.S. armed intervention could also be triggered by a regime breakdown and ensuing civil war on the island. On balance, while these scenarios could not be discounted, the general consensus seemed to be that they were less likely than probable.

VI. Leadership Succession and Regime Transition

Forum participants agreed that Fidel Castro would most likely die in office, rather than surrender his role as the undisputed leader of the Revolution. This view is supported by what is known of Castro's personality and character in which the preservation of his political power and his quest for historical immortality are dominant values. Nevertheless, the participants thought it possible that a leadership change might come sooner rather than later because of the septuagenarian leader's declining health, his public designation of Raúl Castro as his successor, his gaunt appearance during the Papal visit, and the open discussion within the regime itself concerning the succession issue.

There are clear signs over the past year that the regime has been working to ensure that a transition to another regime does not occur in the near-term because of a succession crisis. The leadership is well aware that the death or incapacity of Fidel Castro--who may in fact be terminally ill--could open the way for fundamental system change. The consensus among participants was that the Cuban leadership is working to forestall that possibility.

The Castro brothers and their followers are aware that a succession crisis could result in the rise of reformers to power, the creation of greater political space, and the eventual breakdown or change of the communist system. This occurred in the Soviet Union with Gorbachev's ascendance after Andropov, and in China with the ascendancy of Deng Xiao Ping after Mao's death. In light of this, the government is attempting to carefully manage the succession process so that it does not open the way for a similar type of regime transition. During the Party Congress last October, Raúl Castro was thus designated by Fidel to be his eventual successor. In January, Ricardo Alarcón, President of the National Assembly of People's Power, humbly yet publicly stated that he would be willing to serve as president.

Participants believed that the prospective team of Raúl Castro and Ricardo Alarcón would most probably be able to maintain regime stability. This prospect was considered undesirable for U.S. interests because it would not lead toward liberal democratic

government. However, precisely because this leadership
combination might to be able to ensure continuing stability on the
island, it could also be said to be in the U.S. interest if social
chaos were the alternative in a less well orchestrated succession.

The strength or weakness of a new government could thus be
something of a double-edged sword for U.S. interests: the weaker
the new government is at the time of the succession, the more
susceptible it would be to U.S. pressures for democratic and
market reforms, but such a government would also be less capable
of stemming possible chaos.   If so, then the Raúl Castro-Ricardo
Alarcón team could simultaneously be the "best" and "worst" that
the U.S. might hope for. One participant speculated that the
ideal situation for the United States would surely be one in which
the "price of victory" for the successor government would be the
setting of conditions for its own future undermining. At present,
however, this option does not seem likely.

Because of Raúl Castro's record as a pragmatist and past
supporter of economic reforms, most participants thought that once
in power he might favor more extensive economic reforms, but
certainly not political reforms. Labeled as Cuba's "Balaguer" by
one participant, Alarcón has demonstrated that he knows well how
to manipulate Cuba's public image, particularly with respect to
the United States, and thus he might be able to promote better
relations with this country. No other possible intra-regime
contenders for the top leadership posts were considered by the
participants.

The Revolutionary Armed Forces' support for the new
leadership team appeared a certainty despite the ascendance of a
new generation of leaders within the FAR. Even younger officials
whose personal allegiances and formative experiences are different
from those of the senior officers corps probably would have little
interest in seeing the implementation of changes that might
negatively affect the position of the military as an institution
and their own personal careers. In addition, it was noted that
Raúl Castro continues to command the personal loyalty of much of
the officer corps, and that he probably has garnered additional
respect in recent years for having strengthened the FAR's direct
responsibility for running a number of important economic
enterprises.

Despite U.S. hopes that the military could play a more
proactive role in a transition, there was general consensus that
there is little evidence to suggest that the FAR believes it has
anything to gain by abandoning the regime, particularly if it were
seen to have done so at U.S. instigation. While the FAR is not a
monolithic institution, it is very nationalistic. It has remained
loyal to the Revolution for the past four decades. Prospects for
its continued loyalty under a government headed by Raúl appear
high, especially if its national role were to be expanded, as was
thought likely by some participants.

Participants generally agreed that there is already a degree
of "structural governance" in Cuba today that bodes well for a
managed succession. This includes a relatively stable leadership

that is largely pragmatic. Particularly among the new generation of leaders, there are people who are "populists" in the sense of finding solutions to the every day problems facing ordinary citizens. They are smart, well educated, and politically sophisticated. It was recognized that these individuals have the capacity to govern at the local and provincial levels, if not lead at the national level.

Nonetheless, the recent openness regarding the looming succession problem has created many uncertainties within the government. This is reflected in the increasing cautious behavior of even well established leaders regarding policy issues involving political as well as economic reform, while younger officials are being pressed to prove that they would not be "another Gorbachev." Their uncertainties stem from their not knowing where the line is being drawn regarding expectations and behavior during a period of economic and political flux.

Some participants cautioned that observers of Cuba should be wary of drawing too many analogies from other former communist states. Yet, Fidel Castro has clearly learned a lot from the experiences of the Soviet Union, Eastern Europe, and China, in terms of the mistakes to be avoided if his regime is to survive him. The importance of a careful orchestration of the succession process, and the identification (and presumably, weeding out) of "secret" reformers who might lead the Revolution astray, appear to be among those lessons. Another is the need to have a strong leadership in place as seen by his selection of the Raúl Castro-Ricardo Alarcón team.

VII. Prospects for the Future

In the view of most participants, all these considerations point to regime continuity, with or without Fidel Castro. Though further economic reforms may at some point be implemented, it was expected that the regime would continue to resist the implementation of any substantial political reforms. Nonetheless, the regime is less able now than in the past to continue to resist all change. This is due in part to the forces of decay within the regime itself, as well as to a process underway within society that the state cannot fully control. Hence, the regime over time may find it increasing difficult to "stay the course," and could be obliged to move either in the direction of greater reform or repression. In the interim, the leadership is concentrating on carefully managing a governmental succession that will ensure as much continuity as possible. Based on what is known of the designated successors, there is little reason to expect that they would seek to significantly alter the character of Cuba's present political and economic systems.

III. SESSION II: U.S. INTERESTS AND STAKES IN TRANSITION OUTCOMES

U.S. Interests and Stakes in Cuban Transition Outcomes[*]
by
Phyllis Greene Walker, Forum Rapporteur,
Edward Gonzalez, Forum Organizer, and Richard Nuccio, Forum Advisor

On April 16-17, 1998, RAND convened the second session of its three-part forum on Cuba. The aim of this second session was to consider U.S. interests in Cuba and U.S. stakes in different transition outcomes. The first session, held in February, focused on the current situation on the island and evaluated prospects for change. The final session, to be held in May, will address U.S. policy options. Some forty participants attended the April session, which was held over a day-and-a-half and was off-the-record. Participants included current and former policymakers, Congressional aides and committee staff, intelligence analysts, and academic and other specialists.

Summary

The principal U.S. interest in Cuba is the establishment on the island of a stable, democratic government supported by a free-market economic system. Broad agreement on this overarching policy objective, however, often masked significant differences among participants on many issues.

- *Participants seemed to agree that current U.S. policy is usually reactive and passive.* But they disagreed on whether the emphasis of policy should be to remove the Castro regime as quickly as possible or to support only those policy measures that are likely to encourage a peaceful transition and avoid the involvement of U.S. citizens or forces.

- *Participants agreed in general that impoverished Cuba today offers far less of a conventional military threat to U.S. security interests than a decade ago.* Yet, when the definition of those interests is expanded to include the island's uncontrolled immigration flows, illicit drug trafficking and/or widespread instability, then some participants argued that Cuba's future remains of vital concern to the United States.

- *Participants concurred by and large that measures to reach around the government and to engage the Cuban people directly were desirable.* By strengthening civil society, such policies could hasten a transition that would be more peaceful and democratic in its outcome. However, participants disagreed about whether current policies such as direct flights, authorized remittances, relaxed family travel, and others do more to help the regime than to promote change on the island

- *Most participants agreed on the desirability of the United States working in concert with its allies in Latin America and Europe to develop cooperative, multilateral approaches toward Cuba.* Yet, few participants thought it likely that the United States would be able to make changes in those areas of current U.S. policies to which friends and allies object.

- *Some participants stated that U.S. policy should avoid policies that lead toward unilateral U.S. military involvement or actions that raise the risk of protracted violence on the island.* But others argued that the United States should not forswear any options. They felt that a negotiated settlement between a new Cuban government and former elements of the Castro regime, modeled on the Chamorro government's concessions to the Sandinistas in Nicaragua, should be avoided at all costs.

---

[*] This document is for the exclusive use of Forum participants and should not be distributed to a wider audience.

- *Most participants agreed that U.S. policy should prepare for the possibility that the Castro regime's end may be violent and chaotic, which could entail deliberate or accidental threats to U.S. security.* However, others felt that the United States should do all it could to bring rapid change to the island and that the emphasis on peaceful change was an excuse for inaction.

- *Some participants felt that the United States should sign agreements and work cooperatively with the Cuban government when there are areas of mutual interest on such issues as migration or counternarcotics trafficking, even if such cooperation strengthens the regime's legitimacy.* Others argued that the worst of all outcomes after 40 years of a punishing embargo would be for the United States to adopt policies that might extend the life of a dictatorial regime.

- *Most participants agreed that it was appropriate for U.S. policy to take into account the interests and views of the Cuban-American community.* However, some believed that current U.S. policy heeded only the hard-line element of the community while others argued that the Clinton Administration had mishandled relations with Cuban Americans because of its disdain for these same hard-line leaders.

As seen below, these differences reflect the complexity of Cuba as a foreign policy issue from the standpoint of both realist and moral perspectives.

I. Core and Secondary U.S. Interests in Cuba

The general consensus among the participants was that the principal U.S. interest in Cuba is the popular election of a democratic government supported by a free-market economic system.

The U.S. interest in promoting a democratic Cuba, is consistent with the Clinton Administration's foreign policy objectives for Latin America and the Caribbean, which place democratic government and free trade at the top of U.S. interests in the region. One participant pointed out that although the Clinton Administration has retreated from such a principled stand on its policy toward China, it has committed itself to these values in the Latin American and Caribbean region as a whole. In Cuba, moreover, there are no countervailing business or security interests that override the goal of democratic governance and a market economy on the island.

Disagreement Over the Hierarchy of U.S. Interests

There was considerable debate over the importance of secondary interests or new security concerns, and what their role should be in encouraging Cuba's transition to democracy. While a general consensus existed regarding the primacy of core political, economic, and security-related interests, the participants could not reach agreement on how such newer concerns as human rights, immigration, or the environment, fit into the overall hierarchy of interests. There was also little agreement as to how these traditional and newer interests should be clustered, with several participants defining the clusters of interests differently.

Among the problems identified was whether maintaining a correspondence between means and ends in U.S. policy was necessary for a clear articulation as well as understanding of what U.S. interests are at stake in Cuba. This issue was discussed primarily in reference to the role of values or moral concerns in shaping U.S. policy, as in the case of the embargo, and how those concerns affect other U.S. interests.

There was considerable discussion as to whether current policies, including the long-standing U.S. embargo, may support or undermine the overarching U.S. interest in promoting movement toward a democratic, market-oriented Cuba. Indeed, the overall discussion pointed to a range of problems related to the definition of interests, not least of which was the difficulty of separating out U.S. interests from U.S. policy.

The issue as to whether U.S. interests are better realized by policies that focus on realizing short- as opposed to long-term goals was also addressed. Here the discussion centered on the need for finding a balance between the two, particularly when possible short-term benefits to the Castro regime must be weighed against longer-terms gains for the Cuban people and the United States. Related to this was the question as to how securing specific, or tactical, agreements on lesser priority concerns, such as on immigration or telecommunications, may relate to longer term U.S. interests.

These analytical considerations framed the discussion regarding not only the way that the national interest should be defined with respect to Cuba, but also how it should be realized. As one participant observed, while there was general agreement within the group with respect to the end-goal of a liberal, democratic Cuba, there was a divergence in strategies regarding how to get there.

Contradictory Interests versus Side-Agreements Between the Two Countries

In terms of the relationship between the United States and Castro's Cuba, it was recognized that two immutable, contradictory sets of national interests presently exist that take the form of a zero-sum game. Thus, the U.S. interest in opening up and eventually democratizing Cuba invariably conflicts directly with the Castro regime's primary goal of maintaining its monopoly of political power. This difference is at the core of the problematic relationship between the two countries and explains why U.S. policy has failed to move the regime toward liberalization. Indeed, it was noted that the regime has been so resistant to change that it often seeks to manipulate events in an effort to alter or block U.S. policy goals. This effort includes a willingness to risk not only the lives of Cuban citizens but also U.S. citizens and residents, as reflected in events surrounding the 1994 rafter crisis and the 1996 shoot-down incident.

With respect to the 1994 and 1995 immigration accords that followed the rafter crisis, some participants noted that these side-agreements on regularizing emigration flows have, in effect, provided the regime with a safety valve and with needed remittances from abroad. Ultimately, then, long-term U.S. interests in promoting a transition in Cuba did not appear to have been served by the immigration accord, though it did help assuage more immediate U.S. security concerns raised by the prospect of a new flood of refugees.

According to some, however, side-agreements do not necessarily work against the overarching U.S. interest in promoting a Cuban transition. The challenge lies in identifying the areas of long-term opportunity against possible shorter, adverse term trade-offs.

The telecommunications agreement, for example, helped open up contacts between Cubans and their families and others in the United States. Policymakers deemed that these contacts were more valuable in the long-term than the funds that the Cuban regime receives from the phone calls. Moreover, the agreement was consistent with the effort to open up Cuban society, which is premised on the belief that this will enhance long-term prospects for democracy and a civil society on the island. Some believed that remittances from family members should be viewed similarly. Even though the regime may capture some of the funds, the monies from abroad can help groups become more independent of the state.

Engagement or Lifting the Embargo, and the Question of Promoting Change

Some members pointed out that a similar conflict exists between immediate and longer term interests in the case of those countries that do business with the island. Capital from

Canada, Europe, and Japan is welcomed by the regime, but the investment policies of these countries have had little success in moving the regime toward an economic or political opening. One participant maintained that this failure demonstrates the futility of engagement-type policies because it shows that there is little reason to believe that lifting the U.S. embargo will encourage the regime to embrace a transition toward genuine political and economic change.

On the other hand, some participants maintained that a partial dismantling of the embargo need not be viewed as representing a wholesale surrender to the Castro leadership, but rather as an action fully consonant with U.S. interests. A partial lifting would at least ease the current plight of the Cuban people, which is in the U.S. humanitarian tradition. Equally important, it would be welcomed as a confidence-building step by the regime's more moderate, reformist civilian and military leaders, who may play an important future role in Cuba's democratic transition.

Despite a sharp division over whether the embargo's maintenance remains in the U.S. interest, one participant argued that the end of the Cold War has not provided a justification for the United States to now make peace with a non-democratic Cuba. In a similar vein, another maintained that U.S. policy should not be modified so as to reward Castro. As still another participant put it, the United States should not pursue reconciliation with Latin America's longest lasting dictatorship.

The Issue of Peaceful or Non-Peaceful Change

There was general agreement that it is in the U.S. interest to develop proactive policies aimed at promoting a peaceful democratic transition in Cuba. Indeed, given the regime's propensity to manufacture crises and take the public diplomacy offensive against the U.S. Government, a reactive policy leaves the United States at a decided political disadvantage. On the other hand, one member of the group questioned whether Cuba's democratic transition need be peaceful and warned that such a policy goal could serve as a pretext for inaction--or as a justification for prolonging the life of a communist dictatorship.

However, most participants agreed that the very real possibility of a violent or unsuccessful transition runs counter to U.S. interests, particularly as it might draw the U.S. military into the conflict. Such a contingency was deemed undesirable. Even if "successful" in installing a regime favorable to U.S. interests, a military intervention that resulted in high casualties, and/or in a protracted U.S. occupation of the island, would undermine important U.S. interests in the region. Unlike the U.S. intervention in Haiti, such a step by the United States in Cuba could destroy the new spirit of hemispheric cooperation and the shared goals of democratic governance and free trade.

The Role of U.S. Allies in Promoting Change in Cuba

Many participants believed that involvement of other actors, the European Union, Canada, and Latin America in promoting change in Cuba is to the U.S. advantage. But, one participant maintained that the possibility of such wider engagement is diminished precisely because many U.S. allies see the U.S. position on Cuba as petty, unjustifiable, and morally bereft because it punishes innocent Cubans.

Not everyone was in agreement with this position, however. Earlier, some members even questioned whether some of our allies had the moral authority to condemn U.S. policy given their past behavior in offering weak resistance to Nazi or Soviet aggression, or because of their current as well as past equivocation in actively supporting the democratic cause in the world.

Still, there appeared to be a general acknowledgment that the widespread international perception regarding the weak moral basis of U.S. policy works against U.S. interests. Some noted that a similar lack of understanding regarding the U.S. unwillingness to engage Cuba is also shared among Latin American military officers. No longer considering the Castro regime as a threat, many of their governments have established ties with the Cuban armed forces.

Cuba As a Diminishing National Security Threat

As outlined in the recent Department of Defense report prepared for the Senate Armed Services Committee, the U.S. military no longer views Cuba as a serious threat to U.S. security interests. This reduced threat assessment derives less from a change in the Castro government's posture and intentions vis-à-vis the United States, than from the significant downsizing of the Cuban armed forces, and the sharp degradation of its military arsenal, as a result of the island's continuing economic crisis.

Whether under or after Castro, however, the island still poses a security concern because of the prospect of future illegal migrant surges, the island's potential as a major transshipment base for illegal drug trafficking, and the possible eruption of widespread civil disorder on the island. These are all contingencies that the U.S. military must plan for. For these reasons, and because of its unique geo-strategic properties, the U.S. Naval Base in Guantánamo remains an important military asset in assuring U.S. security interests.

Some participants argued for expanded contacts between U.S. military officers and their Cuban counterparts. This is based on the belief that it would behoove U.S. interests to have such ties in place, given the expectation that the Cuban military will be an important, if not decisive, actor in any transition process. However, the possibility of expanding such contacts needs to be balanced against the concern that they might be seen as conferring U.S. acceptance of the Castro government. This concern suggests the difficulty not only in choosing between short- versus long-term interests, but also in maintaining correspondence among competing U.S. interests.

II. U.S. Stakes in Different Transition Outcomes

A series of eight illustrative, but not necessarily predictive, scenarios were developed and discussed in an effort to identify the possible paths that Cuba's current transition process might follow. By extrapolating from the situation of Cuba of today, the scenarios provided a structured approach for assessing the implications of the different possible transition outcomes for Cuba and for a range of U.S. interests. The scenarios were grouped in three categories:

A. Variations on the Present Situation

The first two scenarios consisted of projections from the current situation on the island. The first was a continuation of the status quo of permanent crisis, with the regime struggling to retain control over society as a post-totalitarian state. The second scenario was characterized by marginal improvements in political and economic conditions as a result of the leadership's introduction of limited reforms, thus enabling the regime to muddle through for the foreseeable future.

Given that the regime's collapse does not appear imminent, most participants considered the two scenarios very plausible. The main questions that they presented for U.S. interests involved whether the United States should simply wait out developments on the island, on the assumption that a situation of permanent crisis could endure for long, or whether it should adopt a proactive role in trying to the move the regime toward further reforms.

As one participant emphasized, the implication of both these scenarios is that the United States must be prepared for the worst, whether in confronting a new migration crisis or even the more remote possibility of a Götterdämmerung-like ending to the regime. In particular, further discussion of the messianic side of Fidel Castro's personality, his potential for irrational action, and his willingness to create crises in order to take the offensive against the United States and/or mobilize support at home, all indicated that such caution is fully warranted.

B. Variations on Instability at the Top on the Heels of Fidel's Illness or Death

In the second category, the setting for both scenarios was altered to encompass variations on leadership instability stemming from the illness or death of Fidel Castro, the worsening of the domestic economic situation, and the continuing erosion of the state's control over society.

In the first scenario, Fidel Castro remains alive, but is unable to rule. Raúl Castro and the armed forces under his command take de facto charge of an interim civil-military government in , which Ricardo Alarcón and a few other civilian leaders are included. In the second scenario, Fidel has died and the military under Raúl takes over the government , which cracks down on the political opposition. But it also implements a program of economic restructuring and reform that offers some hope for Cuba's further evolution toward a market economy. As a result, political stabilization is achieved, but at the cost of renewed repression and authoritarianism.

These scenarios again raised the issue as to whether it is in the U.S. interest to become involved in attempting to effect change--for example, by embracing a policy of engagement with the new government or by refraining from action and contacts until the outcome became clear. The implications for the United States appear to hinge on the longer term prospects for Cuba's movement toward liberal democracy. As one participant observed, a stable, non-democratic regime might offer the worst situation for U.S. interests, precisely because it represents the worst imbalance between the prospects for change in Cuba's future and U.S. interests.

C. Variations on Instability at the Top and from Below Following Fidel's Death

The final category of scenarios encompassed four variations on instability at the top and from below in the wake of Fidel's death. In each of the scenarios, economic deterioration continues and societal pressures for real change build up.

In the first of the four scenarios, Raúl succeeds his brother but his regime soon starts to unravel. It is unable to revive the economy, control the spread of anti-government demonstrations and street violence , or ward-off exile attacks. The island slides toward anarchy and civil war.

The second depicts a less ominous future when Raúl and the military concede to the formation of new government of national reconciliation due to the worsening domestic crisis and mounting international pressures for economic change and a political opening. Although the military remains tied to Raúl and his generals, the new government pledges free and fair multi-party elections.

Proceeding from the second scenario, the third one has the communists under Ricardo Alarcón winning the elections, which has the effect of legitimizing the old, non-democratic regime. Prospects for democracy thus remain dim, while problems with official corruption and drug trafficking ties also bode ill for Cuba's future.

The final scenario has the democratic opposition winning the elections, with the new government moving to build a democratic, market-oriented Cuba. However, the new government must rule without a supportive civil society, while facing serious challenges to its authority from the communist party and the *raulista*-controlled military establishment.

There was little consensus as to which of these four scenarios was more likely to develop. However, there was clear agreement that the first scenario in which the regime unraveled--which one participant described as a "CNN scenario"--was the least desirable for the United States and the one most apt to draw the United States into direct, military involvement.

The second scenario, which offered the prospect of elections, was seen as desirable in that it presented a critical opportunity for the United States to become engaged to support the process of national reconciliation. In this case, one participant judged that should such a situation arise, it was not in the U.S. interest to wait until a pure or definitive outcome was at hand before committing the United States to a policy of engaging the new government. Another pointed out that U.S. embargo had to evaluated with respect to whether it was contributing to the island's destabilization during this critical transition period, or whether it provided the U.S. with leverage for inducing the new government to undertake needed reforms.

With respect to the two possible electoral outcomes, the participants reluctantly agreed that a Nicaraguan-type scenario might well turn out to be the best situation the United States could hope for in a post-Fidel Cuba. As in Nicaragua after 1990, a democratically elected civilian president would try to rule the country even though members of the old regime retain control of the security apparatus. In Cuba's case, however, it was pointed out that civil society would be far weaker than in pre-1990 Nicaragua.

These scenarios prompted discussion over how U.S. policy should respond to developments on the island. Given that the United States does have an important stake in any political outcome in Cuba, the participants agreed that a proactive policy toward Cuba would be in U.S. interests. However, the participants also recognized that in the event of changes in Cuba, a domestic policy debate within the United States over the appropriate course of U.S. action would invariable slow the U.S. ability to respond in a given situation, whether in forestalling further chaos or in supporting a reconciliation process. Nevertheless, this slowing down of the process, some noted, should not be seen so much as an impediment to policy implementation but as a sign that the U.S. system was working.

Within the context of this U.S. policy debate, the role of the Cuban-American community was discussed most extensively. It was suggested that the U.S. administration needs not only to learn how to better respond to the Cuban-American community but also to recognize that there are diverse points of view within it. It was agreed that Cuban-Americans do have an important stake in the domestic debate on Cuba and that their recommendations and interests should be considered in the development of policy toward the island.

IV. SESSION III: U.S. POLICY TOWARD CUBA TODAY AND AFTER CASTRO
Session III of the RAND Forum on Cuba

U.S. POLICY OPTIONS TOWARD CUBA TODAY AND AFTER CASTRO
by
Phyllis Greene Walker, Forum Rapporteur
Edward Gonzalez, Forum Organizer, and Richard Nuccio, Forum
Advisor

On May 28-29, 1998, the third session of RAND's three-part forum on Cuba was convened. The aim of this third session was to consider policy options for dealing with present-day Cuba and a Cuba after Fidel Castro is no longer present. The first session, held in February, focused on the current situation on the island and evaluated prospects for change. The second session considered U.S. interests in Cuba and U.S. stakes in different transition outcomes. Some forty-five participants attended the May session, which was held over a day-and-a-half and was off-the-record. Participants included current and former policymakers, congressional aides and committee staff, intelligence analysts, and academic and other specialists.

SUMMARY

Broad agreement was reached among participants that the principal U.S. policy objectives toward Cuba are to promote the transition to democracy and a market-oriented economy on the island. Although the transition is not likely to take place until after Fidel Castro departs the scene, there was also agreement that United States should help lay its groundwork by shoring up Cuba's emerging civil society, and seeking contacts with the military and younger generation of reformers.

Surprisingly, few participants called for the total lifting of the U.S. embargo. Within the majority favoring the embargo, however, the consensus broke down as to whether it should be maintained in its present form, or eased on a selective or conditional basis.

- Those favoring the present embargo argued that it signals that the United States will not do business with Latin America's longest lasting dictatorship, complicates the Castro regime's chances for economic survival, increases the necessity for economic reforms, and provides the U.S. with leverage for later influencing the transition under a post-Castro government.

- Those critical of the embargo argued that it makes the United States look petty and mean-spirited, hinders people-to-people contacts, does little to strengthen Cuba's nascent civil society, and provides the Castro regime with a scapegoat for its own economic failures and a pretext for clamping down on dissent. They called for more "creative" and "flexible" approaches within present policy and law.

Forum participants voiced strong support for improving the policy process on Cuba through sustained presidential leadership

and attention, resolving the tension between the Administration
and Congress over existing Cuba policy, and attending to the
interests and concerns of the Cuban-American community. The Forum
noted that the issue of property restitution and compensation
needs to be addressed before it becomes an obstacle to Cuba's
eventual democratic transition. The Forum also called for the
formation of a Bipartisan National Commission on Cuba with the aim
of forging a broad policy consensus toward a Cuba under and after
Castro before U.S. policy is overtaken by events on the island.

I. CUBA AND THE CONTEXT OF U.S. POLICY

As with the preceding two Forum sessions, there was general
agreement that real system change in Cuba awaits Castro's passing.
In the meantime, the fact that the Cuban leadership has been able
to survive and "reconstitute" itself after losing its
international support system following the collapse of the Soviet
Union, suggested to most participants that the regime may be
around for the foreseeable future, and that U.S. policy must take
this into account. There was also recognition that Fidel Castro's
departure from power is likely to produce not only great political
uncertainty on the island, but also improved prospects for Cuba's
transition toward democracy and a more market-oriented economy
even if his regime continues in power.

The basic policy question that these assumptions posed for
the Forum was whether it was best for the United States to "stay
the course" by essentially maintaining the embargo, or to modify
U.S. policy with the aim of trying to engage if not the regime,
then the Cuban people themselves, in order to move Cuba toward an
eventual democratic-market transition. As will be seen below,
there was less agreement over which of these approaches would best
help the United States realize its goal of promoting fundamental
political and economic change in Cuba.

There was also disagreement over what considerations need to
be factored into the formulation of U.S. policy. For example,
several participants maintained that current policy remains overly
fixated on Fidel Castro, so much so that it leads to our policy
being premised on a single scenario in which his ouster leads to
change in Cuba. As a result, U.S. policy tends to exclude other
actors and forces who might otherwise be influential in moving
Cuba toward a democratic transition. Some participants also
suggested that the views of those deemed to be "outsiders"--i.e.,
our allies in Europe, Canada, and Latin America--should be weighed
carefully in formulating U.S.-Cuba policy. This inclusion is
particularly needed today, they argued, since the United States is
relatively isolated within the international community on its
stance toward Cuba. The Catholic Church's view should also be
considered because of its "moral authority" in calling for a
change in U.S. policy.

Others disagreed with these views. Current U.S. policy,
they argued, must focus on Fidel Castro because of his continued
dominance of Cuba's polity. Furthermore, U.S. policy not only has

obliged the Castro government to undertake some reforms, but also it has taken the high moral ground because it signals that the U.S. will not compromise with communism and dictatorship. On this issue, U.S. policy ought not to be influenced by criticisms from the international community--no more so than in the 1980s, when the Reagan Administration doggedly pursued a policy toward the U.S.S.R. that was criticized by many of our allies, but which proved to be one that ultimately contributed to the downfall of communism in Eastern Europe and the Soviet Union.

Greater unanimity was reached when the discussion turned to Cuba's internal political dynamics, particularly with respect to laying the groundwork for a future democratic transition. Here, participants concurred on the need for U.S. policy to target several Cuban domestic actors.

The most important of these, it was universally agreed, is Cuba's emerging civil society, which encompasses those institutions, organizations, and groups not affiliated with the government, most of which are also critical of or opposed to the regime.[1] There was general acknowledgment that civil society in Cuba remains "incipient": Whereas the Catholic Church and its affiliated international relief organization, Caritas, stand out as genuine non-governmental organizations, the Cuban state has sought to suppress, penetrate, or co-op most other NGOs, while arresting and harassing individual dissidents and human rights activists. Yet, elements of a nascent civil society are present, including in the small, struggling private sector. They need to continue to be supported and protected by the international community because they are essential to Cuba's future democratic transition.

Some participants felt that the Catholic Church's efforts to "open political space" since the Papal visit last January may help other civil society actors over time. However, there was general recognition that much depends on how much of an opening the government is willing to tolerate and here the signs are not terribly encouraging. This makes it all the more necessary, participants agreed, that U.S. policy should continue giving highest priority to nurturing the growth and development of Cuba's fledgling civil society.

Another domestic actor requiring special U.S. attention, it was agreed, is the Cuban military. While the Revolutionary Armed Forces (FAR) gained international recognition due to its military incursions in Africa in the 1970s and 1980s, it has emerged with greater domestic influence over the past eight years or so as a result of Cuba's economic crisis. This new role for the FAR has been accompanied by greater delegation of authority to its generals over recent years.

---

[1]Since the early 1990s, Cuba's civil society includes: the Catholic and Protestant churches, Catholic relief organizations, self-help groups, private entrepreneurs, independent associations of workers, journalists, and economists, and dissidents and human rights activists and their respective organizations.

In acknowledging the military's more prominent role, there was general agreement concerning the desirability of promoting military-to-military contacts between the United States and Cuba. Even on an informal basis, these contacts would serve as a confidence-building mechanism that could help forestall possible conflict between the two countries. Perhaps more importantly, informal contacts would provide the United States with an avenue of communication to what is likely to be a pivotal if not preeminent Cuban institution in any post-Castro transition process.

Another suggestion was that U.S. policy promote broader U.S. contacts with mid-level government technocrats, especially the reformers among them, because they are likely to assume greater influence and importance during a future transition. However, the practical means to engage this latter group, especially if done by means of contacts through the U.S. Interests Section in Havana, were judged to be limited at this time.

II. POLICY OPTIONS TOWARD CUBA

Though weakened, Cuba's communist state remains the dominant actor notwithstanding the infusion of foreign capital into the island and the reemergence of a small private sector and a nascent civil society. Hence, as emphasized by several participants, change in Cuba is not likely to be determined by outside actors as evidenced by the failure of both the 36-year-old U.S. embargo and the policy of engagement pursued by the Canadians and Europeans.

Nevertheless, what to do about the U.S. embargo became the Forum's most contentious policy issue even though only a few participants called for the embargo's lifting all together. Whereas most participants appeared to favor retaining some form of the embargo, this majority view immediately split into two main camps--one for essentially keeping the embargo in present form, the other for modifying or "tinkering" with it.

Option 1: Maintaining the Embargo

Those who advocated maintaining the embargo argued that it should not be significantly changed--much less abandoned--at this time:

1. *The embargo signals the commitment of the United States to seeing democracy, a market system, and human rights take hold in a country that stands as the last redoubt of communism in the West.* To lift the embargo now would signify that we are prepared to accommodate a communist dictatorship in Cuba at a time when the rest of Latin America is moving, however haltingly, toward democratic capitalism.

2. The embargo complicates the Castro government's ability to function by making it more difficult for Cuba to obtain foreign investments, and international loans and credits. Were the embargo lifted now, no matter if only partially, the Castro government would directly benefit through the infusion of new investments, loans, and credits from Canada and Europe, as well as from the United States. Additionally, any weakening of the embargo would be tantamount to succumbing to the Castro regime's disinformation campaign that exploits humanitarian concerns over the island's food and medicine shortages.

3. The embargo provides the United States with a measure of leverage for increasing the pressure on the Cuban government to liberalize the island's polity and economy. Without the embargo, the government would have less incentive to embrace change. Moreover, while embargoes in general may not be particularly effective in promoting system change, they can help channel and accelerate such change once it is underway. Hence, after Fidel Castro is gone, the prospect of lifting the embargo can be used as leverage by the U.S. government to help influence the transition even if the present communist regime survives his passing. Abandoning the embargo at this time would thus be folly.

Option 2. Lifting the Embargo Unconditionally

Although only a minority of participants thought it was time to abandon the embargo entirely, they and the selective or conditional lifters shared a number of assumptions regarding the present embargo. As voiced by the unconditional lifters, these were as follows:

1. The embargo's ineffectiveness in bringing down the regime during the past thirty-six years in itself is sufficient evidence to indicate that it will continue to be ineffective in the future. Hence, it is time for the United States to try new initiatives that could better help promote a peaceful transition in Cuba.

2. Dropping the embargo would remove Castro's excuse that the United States is responsible for Cuba's problems, and neutralize the regime's efforts to equate political dissent and opposition with treason. By lessening the U.S. threat perception, greater political space could become available for such human rights activists as Elizardo Sánchez, who has been critical of both the regime and the embargo.

3. Lifting the embargo would help open Cuba up through the resulting infusion of American dollars, businessmen, professionals, students, and tourists. Such an infusion would influence Cuban values, reinforce civil society actors, and weaken the state's grip over society. It would set in motion forces that the regime could not fully control.

4. Lifting the embargo would serve to lessen the isolation of the United States within the international community. The United States would cease being viewed as being "petty" and "mean-spirited." No longer accused by its critics of being "the bully on the block," the United States would raise its moral standing in the eyes of the world.

Especially as framed by the unconditional lifters, some of the above assumptions were refuted by those favoring the retention of the embargo. Some argued that there is little historical evidence to support the assumption that economic and other linkages with the West are in themselves sufficient to produce the kind of changes expected from the infusion of dollars and American tourists into Cuba. On the contrary, despite being integrated into the world economy, authoritarian states existed for decades in Latin America starting in the 1960s, as well as in Asia and China today. Others noted that since the policy of engagement pursued by Canada and the Europeans has been no more effective in moving Cuba toward a transition than has U.S. policy, there is little basis for believing that lifting the embargo would succeed where the policy of engagement has failed.

Option 3: Lifting the Embargo Selectively or Conditionally

The majority of those critical of the embargo favored a selective or conditional lifting the embargo, or, in the parlance of the meeting, "tinkering" with it. While sharing most of the assumptions of the unconditional lifters, they differed in favoring a partial retention of the embargo for the time being, and in stressing the needs of the Cuban citizenry. Essentially, they called for either the embargo's selective or conditional lifting for the purpose of influencing the political situation on the island over the long-term on the basis of the following arguments:

1. *The embargo should exclude the provision of humanitarian assistance.* The inclusion of food and medicine in the embargo was characterized by one critic as reflecting a degree of pettiness that is "morally unbecoming of a great power." Participants were also reminded that food and medicines were excluded during the embargo's early years, thereby providing a precedent for their exclusion now. Such a step would be a humanitarian policy that addresses the needs of the Cuban people who are the innocent victims of the Castro government's retrograde policies, and its efforts to use the food and medicine issue for propaganda purposes.

However, neither of the two pending humanitarian bills before Congress--the Cuban Solidarity Act submitted by Senator Jesse Helms and the Dodd-Torres Bill--received strong support from the Forum. The Helms legislation was roundly criticized as essentially a "non-starter" because of its imposition of requirements and conditions that Cuban NGOs administering the assistance--not to speak of the Cuban government--would find impossible to accept. For its part, the Dodd-Torres Bill was not deemed realistic because Cuba lacks the financial means for purchasing medical and food supplies from the United States.

In rebuttal, several participants noted that the regime itself deprives its citizenry of access to state-controlled medical supplies. They are reserved for the *nomenklatura* and hard-currency paying foreigners who are lured to Cuba under the government's program of "medical tourism." While the health tourism industry grows, average Cubans do without. In their view, the ideal way to ship food and medicines is not by lifting the embargo on those items, but through licensed donations and gift packages as permitted under present U.S. law. That way, the goods are distributed directly to the Cuban people, or through such non-governmental intermediaries as Caritas, rather than falling into the hands of the Cuban government. As one participant put it, the U.S. Government must not participate in "subsidizing the repression of the Cuban people," which would inevitably result from even partially lifting the embargo.

A separate issue discussed by the participants was the treatment of sales of medicine under existing legislation. Those opposed to lifting the ban sales argued that the 1992 Cuban Democracy Act (CDA) permits sales of medicines to Cuba if certain conditions are met by the Cuban government. They further contended that the regime itself has not pursue the possibilities of obtaining licensed sales in order to continue its propaganda campaign against the U.S. embargo. However, those supporting some form of sales stated that the language of the CDA was designed to discourages sales of medicines by conditioning such sales in such as way as to make it politically unacceptable to the Cuban government to seek licenses and too complicated for U.S. companies and NGOs desiring licenses.

Indeed, how to help the Cuban people without benefiting the regime posed a perplexing issue for several participants. One warned that the Cuban government would be "picking up dollars at some point," including through the resale of the imported items. Another voiced concern that the United States would find it politically difficult to "hold the line" to just food and medicines because U.S. corporations would take advantage of any opening in the embargo to push for its complete dismantling. If Eli Lilly can sell medicines to Cuba, it was noted, then John Deere will press to sell tractors for food production.

2. *The embargo should not place U.S. policy in a straight-jacket but allow for "creativity" and "flexibility."* Despite the differences over the embargo, there was general acceptance of the view that an effort should be made to look for "running room" within the parameters of current policy and law in order to craft a "more creative" and "flexible" policy approach. To this end, steps could be taken under current law to help promote greater people-to-people contacts, increase information flows, buttress civil society actors, and strengthen entrepreneurial values and skills in Cuba society.

Starting with the more modest measures, these steps would include easing current strictures on remittances, allowing expanded travel for cultural or academic exchanges, and establishing management training programs to support private entrepreneurial development. Besides lifting restrictions on food and medicine, bolder steps could be taken at the higher end of the policy spectrum that would require changes in the embargo. These might include relaxing the restrictions on all travel; allowing U.S. selective investments in such key sectors as health or food production; and loosening U.S. restrictions on the exportation of information technology. It was also suggested that even certain excess U.S. government commodities, such as pediatric medical supplies or incubators, could be made available if the means were found to prevent the Cuban government from reselling the items.

Ideally, the policy options resulting from such creative thinking would help the United States achieve closer relations with the Cuban people without "blessing the regime." However, skepticism was voiced as to whether such fine-tuning was possible in Cuba. It was pointed out that the Cuban government is in a position to reap a large share of the incoming dollars because of the central role the state continues to play in the economy, including in the external, foreign-exchange producing sector.[2]

3. *Conditional lifting of the embargo in response to the adoption of liberalizing policies by the Cuban government.* The U.S. government, it was proposed by some, should establish "a more reasonable posture" with respect to conditional engagement toward the present government in order to promote change.[3] This would entail limited, calibrated changes in the embargo as a means of encouraging--or responding to--the regime's adoption of liberalizing measures. The United States should appear reasonable, one participant argued, without being so specific as to have a list of how it would respond to the Cubans. Loosening the embargo, another noted, could trigger a dynamic, unpredictable reaction within the Cuban elite, especially among those leaders in their 30s and 40s.

The United States should thus attempt to exercise tactical flexibility in the short-term in support of its long-term strategic aim of moving Cuba toward a more democratic, market-oriented system, and the protection of human rights. Otherwise, it was argued, "many opportunities" to influence events and society are being missed and we are wrongly isolating Cubans from Americans. Flexibility may be all the more important in dealing with so personalistic a regime as that headed by Fidel Castro: if we are to put such a regime on the defensive, we must find ways "to show that the emperor has no clothes." As stated by a

---

[2]Most foreign investments take the form of joint enterprise arrangements between the foreign investor and the Cuban state, including tourist resorts, hotels and other facilities. Also, Gaviota is a military-run enterprise that runs a far-flung network of tourist facilities and services.

[3]One participant went so far as to suggest that a "sunset" provision could even be established that would set a date for the embargo's expiration, regardless of the political situation on the island.

participant who favored calibrated change, "the value of sanctions is in setting the price of removing them."

While at times there was support for some of the above proposals and sentiments, there was no general agreement on the wisdom of conditional lifting at this time. In the eyes of some, there are no more signs today that the Castro government is prepared to either initiate liberalizing measures or respond positively to a "calibrated response" by Washington, than was true of the early-to-mid-1990s when the policy was attempted. Although it was left unstated, the general feeling may have been that a partial or conditional lifting of the embargo would be most effective once Fidel Castro passes from the scene.

IV. THE ISSUE OF PROPERTY RESTITUTION AND COMPENSATION

Because of the concern over the potential divisiveness of the property issue on Cuba's eventual democratic transition, there was agreement that the question of compensation and restitution needs to be addressed well before such a transition begins. The issue is important, it was asserted, because many Cubans on the island fear they will be the losers when the regime ends and members of the Cuban-American community return to lay claim to their old properties. For that reason, the property issue looms as a major stumbling block if Cuban-Americans push for restitution.

At the same time, it was pointed out that this is an issue in which non-governmental organizations in the Cuban-American community could play a constructive role in helping lower expectations within the community over future restitution. As one participant stated, "too much time has passed" for there to be a "wholesale restitution of property." But another objected to the notion that anything less than a return of disputed property to its original owners would be acceptable. Such a stance would convey a lack of seriousness regarding the commitment of the United States to democracy and the free market. An expropriation is legal, another countered, as long as compensation is "just and adequate."

Given the importance that this issue may assume when a transition does occur, it was suggested that taking steps now to establish government-to-government contacts to address conflicting property claims might be a good idea. Another participant disagreed, insisting that the U.S. government should not become directly involved in mediating this issue. Hence, as with the embargo, there thus appeared to be a general consensus regarding the importance of the compensation and restitution issue, but less agreement over the specific policies the United States should follow.

V. MEASURES TO IMPROVE THE POLICY PROCESS

There was broad recognition among participants that certain aspects of the policy process itself contributed greatly to the ineffectiveness of our present Cuba policy. Of particular note were the tensions and difficult relations that exist between the executive and legislative branches of government with respect to Cuba. While to some extent institutional friction is to be expected, many noted that the difficulties that have arisen in the formulation of our Cuba policy appear to be especially excessive, especially when they lead to a virtual deadlock over policy. These differences have been exacerbated by what one participant on the Congressional side candidly described as an atmosphere of "mutual distrust" between Congress and the White House.

With respect to the executive branch, several individuals argued that the President needs to reassert his authority and assume greater responsibility for the conduct of U.S. policy toward Cuba. It was pointed out that the President's latitude in setting Cuba policy has been limited ever since he "signed away" his authority to change the embargo with the Helms-Burton Law. Still, there was general agreement that the President could and should do more than he's been doing.

In particular, U.S. Cuba policy should be made a specific *and* sustained focus of presidential attention. Questions regarding our Cuba policy should not be addressed in off-hand statements, as happened with the remarks the President made during the visit to Washington of the Italian Prime Minister earlier this year. To be sure, there are competing foreign policy interests that frequently divert the President's attention. But, as one participant observed, it is especially important for the President to recognize that he needs to remain attentive to the Cuban issue: Cuba is was one of the two countries in this hemisphere the other being Mexico--where a crisis could "bring down" his presidency.

Notwithstanding the constraints on presidential action established by Helms-Burton, several participants expressed the view that there still was considerable "running room" within the confines of the current law for initiatives toward Cuba. There remains a "tremendous amount of flexibility" under Helms-Burton. However, the difficulty in moving forward with new initiatives lies in the fact that they would require sustained presidential attention both in developing and implementing the new policies.

Within the legislative branch, it was noted that there exists a perception that the Administration has sought to limit or even exclude Congressional input in the formulation of Cuba policy. This has led to the development of considerable resentment and suspicion within Congress regarding the Administration's real intentions. This perception in itself indicates that the Administration needs to work more closely with Congress in order to improve relations and develop an effective policy. As one participant pointed out, however, we are faced with a dilemma in our Cuba policy because the short-term pay-offs in U.S. domestic politics related to Cuba tend to run counter to U.S. long-term interests regarding the island.

How to move beyond this asymmetry of interests in order to find "common ground" for setting U.S. policy occupied the Forum's attention during much of the second morning. Here, there appeared to be broad agreement, even among those whose views diverged on other policy issues, regarding the importance of working together for a common end.

One suggestion was that the Administration adopt a less confrontational stance toward the members of Congress who support differing policy approaches to Cuba, a stance that might lead them to become more cooperative. This should include efforts to bolster contacts with those members of Congress who represent the interests of the Cuban-American community--a constituency that should, it was agreed, have a voice in the formulation of U.S.-Cuba policy. In a statement that suggested the need for greater accommodation and cooperation among all, one participant suggested that it would be a "good deal" for Cuban-Americans and the United States if the Cuban-American community was willing to "swap its hard-line stance for a policy supported by mainstream America."

Nevertheless, without efforts to improve executive-legislative relations, another observed, we can get either a Cuba policy that the administration does not want to implement (as with Helms-Burton), or a policy that the Congress attacks. In neither case does the United States obtain a realistic, workable policy that would be effective in promoting U.S. interests.

VI. A BIPARTISAN NATIONAL COMMISSION ON CUBA

To break the institutional impasse and advance the policy debate over Cuba, there was broad agreement on "looking beyond Fidel Castro"--at how the United States can support Cuba's future transition toward a more democratic, market-oriented society. Here, there was strong support for the recommendation that the President and Congress establish a Bipartisan National Commission on Cuba modeled after the National Bipartisan Commission on Central America.

Like the Kissinger Commission fifteen years ago, the Cuba commission could provide the venue in which to air divergent policy views on Cuba today, and forge a broader consensus for a future policy toward a Cuba without Castro. Such a commission could help move us toward the realization of the U.S. long-term interest, which, as characterized by one participant, entailed not only the promotion of democracy, but also the development of a "humane, liberal society" in Cuba. Unlike with the Kissinger Commission, however, the commission on Cuba ought to be set up before there are crises or other events on the island that could overtake U.S. policy.

    In this respect, the Forum ended on a hopeful note: The fact
that the policy divisions in the Forum's last session were less
intense than was originally anticipated, suggests that a National
Bipartisan Commission on Cuba might well be able to reach a policy
consensus and craft policy recommendations toward Cuba that would
generate broad support within the American policymaking community
and public at large.

V. THE CUBAN CONUNDRUM

by

Edward Gonzalez, Forum Organizer, and
Richard A. Nuccio, Forum Advisor[*]

On January 5, 1999, six months after The RAND Forum on Cuba held its last session, the Clinton Administration announced changes in U.S.-Cuba policy. The measures, though modest, were significant because they signaled a return of the Clinton Administration's Cuba policy to the path it was on before the February 1996 shootdown of two U.S. civilian planes piloted by Cuban American exiles.

Unlike the Helms-Burton legislation passed in the political crisis provoked by the shootdown, the recent Clinton measures make no pretense of being intended to overthrow the Castro regime. Instead they focus longer term--to help Cuban society prepare for a post-Castro era in which a more open polity and economy is presumed to be possible. This is the long-range U.S. policy objective that the Forum had repeatedly advised, beginning with its first session in February. However, the Administration did not accept another of the Forum's recommendations, first endorsed in its May session, and independently seconded by a range of Republican Senators and former foreign policy officials this past fall, that the President appoint a national bipartisan commission to review U.S.-Cuba policy.

Reactions to the Administration's initiatives and its rejection of the commission reveal a lot about the policy environment surrounding Castro's Cuba. Leading anti-Castro circles in the Cuban-American community were restrained in their criticism of the new initiatives in part because the White House had rejected the idea of a Cuba commission. Both proponents and

---

[*] Although the authors organized and led The RAND Forum on Cuba, and have based many of their comments on its deliberations, the views that follow are their own and do no necessarily represent the views of Forum participants.

opponents of the commission had assumed that its main recommendation would be the unilateral lifting of some core elements of the U.S. embargo. Critics of current policy, on the other hand, predictably labeled the initiatives timid or irrelevant. Their preferred policy alternative is to have the embargo lifted in whole or in part.

These divergent positions show how polarized the Cuba debate remains within the American body politic and how little maneuvering room the Executive Branch has in fashioning a policy toward Cuba, which already is constrained by Helms-Burton. At the same time, the two opposing camps seem to share a similar premise in believing that the U.S. embargo determines the course of Cuban politics. As will be argued below, both of these positions are out of touch with the island's political realities and are oblivious to the trade-offs that the United States must weigh in dealing with Cuba. Most of all, critics of present policy are wrong in holding American policy, not the Castro government, responsible for Cuba's failure to change. Finally, all sides to the debate seem to share a complacency about the need for rapid change in Cuba. For, although the Cuban people will suffer the most, the longer Cuba's transition is delayed, the greater the likelihood it will be violent, with important U.S. interests and concerns being imperiled.

THE FRACTIOUS POLICY ENVIRONMENT

The political conditions that led to passage of the Helms-Burton bill and its signing into law by the President in March 1996 began to change more than a year ago. That was when the papal visit to Cuba transformed the political climate internationally and within the United States. The Pope's criticism of the embargo and, more significantly, his demonstration that he could maintain his principled support for democracy and human rights while making concessions to the regime, mobilized opposition to Helms-Burton and to the embargo, its centerpiece. However, the opposition this time came not just from the usual liberal and leftist quarters,

but also from conservatives and the business community. In an
October 13, 1998 letter, Senator John W. Warner (R-VA) was joined
by fourteen other Republican and Democratic co-signers, the
majority of whom had voted for Helms-Burton, in urging the
President to appoint a National Bipartisan Commission on Cuba to
review U.S. policy. Warner's initiative had earlier been
encouraged by other former distinguished Republican officials.[4]
All the Congressional and former Executive Branch notables shared
the assumption that the U.S. economic embargo against Cuba is a
demonstrable failure.[5]

The proposed Cuba commission immediately came under fire
from Cuban-American Congressional representatives and the Cuban-
American National Foundation. Strongly supportive of Helms-Burton,
they view the embargo principally as a way to deny the Castro
government needed capital with which to shore up its rule. They
charged that several of the former Republican officials represent
business interests eager to invest in and trade with Cuba, and
thus viewed the proposal as a Trojan Horse in which American
capital would end by rescuing Cuban communism.[6]

As was noted, the Administration did not adopt the Cuba
commission proposal. Instead, it responded to the pressures
unleashed by the papal trip, and the Republican initiative for
changes in U.S. Cuba policy, by adopting many of the
recommendations offered by a Task Force of the Council on Foreign

---

[4] A follow-up December 11 letter gained an additional four
Republican co-signers and five Democrats. Prior to the original
letter, Senator Warner had been encouraged to submit his letter by
former Secretary of State Lawrence S. Eagleburger in a letter
supported, among others, by former Secretaries of State Henry A.
Kissinger and George P. Shultz, former Secretary of State Frank
Carlucci, and former Senate Majority Leader Howard H. Baker.

[5] See William D. Rogers, "Why Keep a lonely Stance on Cuba?"
The Los Angeles Times, November 13, 1998. Rogers was Assistant
Secretary and Under-Secretary of State in the Ford Administration,
1974-1977.

[6] See Jorge Más Santos, "Aim at Cuba's freedom, not money,"
The Miami Herald, November 30, 1998.

Relations headed by Bernard Aronson and William Rogers.[7] One important Task Force recommendation that was not publicly endorsed, however, was that the United States begin military-to-military contacts with Cuba's Revolutionary Armed Forces--a recommendation which the Forum had also made.

The initiatives that were adopted by the Administration are aimed at increasing the flow of dollars, goods, information, and Americans into Cuba for the purpose of strengthening the island's incipient civil society and rendering individual Cubans less dependent on the state. Thus, any U.S. resident, not just those with family members in Cuba, will now be able to send up to $1,200 a year to Cuban families. Charter passenger flights to Cuba will be increased not only from Miami but from other U.S. cities as well, and to Cuban cities besides Havana. The Administration will offer again to establish direct mail service between the two countries.[8] Additionally, the sale of food and agricultural goods to individual Cubans and legitimate NGOs on the island are now authorized, and the sale of medicines will be increased and the licensing process greatly expedited.

These are creative extensions of the "Track II" policies of the 1992 Cuban Democracy Act that the Forum had urged as well. As occurred with Track II, they attempt "to reach around the Cuban government to the Cuban people," while appealing to the Cuban American community's impulse to help their less fortunate brethren on the island. However, they also share the defects of past Track II policies: Because they are correctly and unavoidably perceived as challenges to their regime, Castro and other Cuban leaders have the incentive and the means to delay, deform, or prohibit their implementation.

----

[7] For a summary of the Task Force recommendations, see Bernard W. Aronson and William D. Rogers, "Bringing Cuba in From the Cold," *The New York Times*, January 2, 1999. A29.
[8] Cuba had previously conditioned mail service on commercial flights. The frequency and diverse destination of the authorized charters under the new initiatives now offers Cuba a reasonable compromise if it wants to take it.

More ardent anti-Castro circles in and outside the Cuban-
American community found the policy aim of the Administration's
initiatives to be illusory--as had earlier been the case with some
of the Forum participants. They doubt that civil society can be
strengthened, truly independent NGOs found, or the grip of
Castro's totalitarian state significantly weakened, by more
Americans, food and medicine, and cash remittances flowing into
Cuba. They argue that the estimated $500 million to $800 million
in annual remittances currently going into Cuba ultimately
strengthen the Cuban state because of the latter's ability to
capture dollars circulating on the island through its dollar-only
stores.

These arguments, however, fail to recognize that Cuba's
current political reality imposes policy trade-offs that are often
less than ideal. Uncertain but anticipated long-term gains toward
the goal of a peaceful, democratic transition in Cuba may, with
greater certainty, entail set-backs for that same objective over
the shorter-term. For example, the latest initiatives aim at
providing assistance to individuals and NGOs in the hope they
eventually may be strengthened vis-a-vis the Cuban state. The
downside, however, is that the government is certain to gain over
the short-term by having additional food, medicine, and dollars
enter the economy.

This is not an abstract debate. There is no question that
the decision to expand long distance phone service with Cuba has
contributed, among other important gains, to the growth of an
independent journalists movement on the island, even as the
government gained from the new infusion of dollars. Similarly,
the encouragement of humanitarian donations under the Cuban
Democracy Act provided the material foundation for the growth of
Caritas, the Catholic Church's humanitarian agency, even though
the donations helped make social tensions more manageable for the
government.

Liberal and conservative opponents of present U.S. policy
were no more charitable in their response to the Administration's

new initiatives. Gillian Gunn Clissold pointed out they were unlikely to benefit most Cubans who lack the dollars with which to buy food and medicines from the United States. She further noted that the Cuban government would hardly approve the implementation of measures that were patently designed to weaken if not subvert the regime, as revealed by its "repetition of 'Track Two' language."[9] Wayne S. Smith accused the White House of having caved in to right-wing Cuban-American pressures in rejecting the proposed commission on Cuba because such a commission would certainly have recommended that our "failed policy" toward Cuba be replaced by the embargo's lifting and direct dealings with the Castro regime. "If we want to encourage the [Castro] government to move ahead with reforms," he concluded, "we must deal with that government."[10] In a blistering op-ed piece, William Ratliff and Roger Fontaine opined that, "None of the proposed changes are unwelcome; they are just either trivial or contradictory, and patently Democratic Party presidential ploys."[11]

Whether or not our present policy has "failed" is an arguable proposition, particularly in light of some of its alternatives as will be discussed later on. In any event, most critics seem to share three underlying assumptions concerning Cuba and U.S. policy:

- First, however halting it may be, Cuba is undergoing a process of system change comparable to the transitions that gripped post-Maoist China, Gorbachev's Soviet Union, and post-1987 Vietnam.

- Second, current U.S. policy toward Cuba is driven primarily if not exclusively by domestic politics because of the influence of the right-wing Cuban-American community, and

---

[9] Gillian Gunn Clissold, "Reaching Out but Not Touching Cubans," *Los Angeles Times*, January 8, 199, B9.

[10] Wayne S. Smith, "Instead of Needed Changes, Administration Continues a Failed Policy," *Los Angeles Times*, January 10, 1999, M2.

[11] William Ratliff and Roger Fontaine, "Cuba, Gore & Campaign 2000," *Union Tribune*, January 17, 1999.

the importance of Florida and New Jersey as key electoral states.

- Third, whereas our present confrontational and punitive policy serves as a brake on Cuba's transition, a more conciliatory policy would help accelerate economic and political reforms in that country.

These assumptions are questionable. They are not grounded in Cuba's current reality. They oversimplify a complex policy issue. And they presume that a changed U.S. policy can only have a positive impact on Castro's Cuba.

CUBA'S STALLED DEMOCRATIC TRANSITION

One of the Forum's key findings, on which there was virtually universal agreement, is that Cuba's leadership today is *not* committed to fundamental system change. To be sure, Cuba has ceased to be the totalitarian state it once was as the state itself was severely weakened by the collapse of the Soviet Union in 1991, and by the economic contraction that followed whereby Cuba's gross national product declined by perhaps as much as 40 percent by 1994 compared to 1989. The consequence is that today's Cuba differs from the Cuba of a decade ago: Because of the acute economic crisis, the government has been obliged to open up the island to foreign investors and tourists, dollarize the economy, and permit self-employment by Cubans in trades, crafts, and services.

Nevertheless, Cuba has yet to enter the stage of system transition. It thus differs substantially from not only the former East European communist states, but also current Asian communist models. With Castro in the lead, Cuba continues to resist fundamental economic reforms. This stands in contrast to communist China where Deng Xiaoping opened up the economy starting two decades ago, and Vietnam where economic liberalization commenced in the late 1980s. Unlike in those two countries, the Castro government's liberalizing reforms so far have amounted to

tactical concessions that can be withdrawn or modified as has
happened with self-employment. They do not signify permanent
structural change imbedded in law and the constitution.

That Cuba today is characterized by stasis is seen by the
commanding role of the state. The state controls Cuba's economy
to a greater degree than in the economies of not only communist
China and Vietnam today, but also Poland, Hungary, and
Czechoslovakia in the 1980s. Foreign investors must contract with
the state, and are required to enter into joint ventures with the
government, including in the highly lucrative tourist industry.
The state operates dollar-only shops to capture the hard-currency
spent by foreigners and by Cubans spending their remittances. A
military enterprise called Gaviota runs a far-flung complex of
tourist resorts and services. The sugar industry is under the
command of the military and a high-ranking Army General. And
rather than dismantle or privatize them, the state continues to
operate inefficient state-enterprises in order not to worsen
unemployment or underemployment.

In contrast, the regime has begun to squeeze the small,
legalized private sector activities that in recent years it
permitted to exist in designated trade, craft and service sectors
of the economy. Cubans who are licensed to be "self-employed" in
these sectors have become more tightly circumscribed and regulated
than in the mid-1990s, with some previously legalized activities
now being closed to private entrepreneurs. Fearing competition
for state restaurants and hotels, and intensified socio-economic
inequalities, Cuban authorities are using confiscatory tax
policies to eliminate certain business activities or prevent their
owners from becoming a prosperous, independent middle class. As a
consequence, the number of legally self-employed Cubans who
operate small, family-run "Mom and Pop" stores, repair shops,
taxies, and *paladares* (home restaurants), has dropped from over
200,000 self-employed in 1996 to just over 160,000 at the end of
1998. After studying Cuba's private sector closely, Philip Peters
thus observes that with respect to the government's policy on

self-employment, "They've let everything play out, but they have not added any new openings. Certainly, there is no interest in letting it expand, at least not immediately."[12]

In the political sphere, the state remains as arbitrary and repressive as ever, notwithstanding the plea by Pope John Paul II. A year after the Pope's January 1998 visit, Fidel Castro celebrated his regime's fortieth anniversary in power, giving him the dubious distinction of being Latin America's longest lasting dictator. The Communist Party monopolizes political power and brooks no opposition, peaceful or otherwise. Pluralism is not tolerated, much less promoted by the state. As José Miguel Vivanco of Human Rights Watch in the Americas has noted, "The harassment against dissidents, human rights activists or anyone else attempting to exercise the most basic rights of association and expression continues exactly the same."[13]

Because of its unique position and resources, the Catholic Church stands out as the only independent institution in Cuba that has been able to garner a bit more space for itself.[14] The government has granted some limited concessions to the Church in the year since the Pope's visit, including selected access to the general population through a few radio stations, but they came only as a result of hard bargaining between the Church and government authorities. Otherwise, the state continues to control the media and access to the Internet, while hampering the rise of non-governmental bodies. As a consequence, Cuba's civil society remains in a state of infancy.

---

[12]As quoted by Larry Rohter, "As the World Takes a New Look, It's the Same Old Cuba," *The New York Times*, January 17, 199, Sec.4:4.

[13]As quoted in *ibid.*

[14]Cuba's Catholic Church not only enjoys a mass following, but also has two unique advantages in negotiating with the government. Like the Cuban state, it is a hierarchical, centralized institution; and it has an international support system through its ties to the Vatican, and to the Catholic Church in the United States, Europe, and Latin America.

40

IMPLICATIONS FOR U.S. POLICY

What does all this signify for Cuba and U.S. policy? As the Forum concluded, *cambio con Fidel*--change with Fidel--is currently an oxymoron. The *Comandante* appears determined not to reverse course, much less undo everything he has stood and fought for, because to do so would undermine the historical role and legacy he was determined to realize even before he took power in 1959. This may mean that fundamental system change in Cuba will have to await his passing from the scene or the weakening of his grip on power.

Indeed, Cuba's transition seems to be condemned to follow the course of transitions in the Soviet Union and China where there were indigenous revolutions and where the departure of the "great leader" like Stalin, or the founding, charismatic "Great Helmsman" like Mao, was the essential precondition that opened the way for system change. Only then can a reformist leader like a Deng Xiaoping or a Gorbachev emerge and form a bloc of supportive followers.[15]

In the meantime, in the early and mid-1990s, Cuba's socialist *caudillo* grudgingly accepted only a limited number of liberalizing economic measures necessary to arrest the economy's freefall. Once the economy showed signs of recovery, deeper reforms were halted, while regime reformers were silenced and marginalized by 1996. As the seventy-two year-old Castro told his audience in his January 1, 1999 speech commemorating the 40th anniversary of the revolution, Cuba continues to be led by someone "who dresses the same, who thinks the same, who dreams the same" as when he came down from the Sierra Maestra on January 1, 1959.

This being the case, no one should be under the illusion that the United States, Canada, the European Union, the Pope, or the Spanish King can persuade Castro to champion reforms anew. As

---

[15]For a further elaboration of this and other points regarding the experiences of other former communist states as they relate to Cuba, see Edward Gonzalez and Thomas S. Szayna, *Cuba and Lessons from Other Communist Transitions--A Workshop Report*, Santa Monica, Calif., RAND, CF-142, 1998.

he made abundantly clear in his January 1, 1999 speech, he sees
himself as the keeper of the faith--as the singular leader who not
only will prevent the return of capitalism and its evil ravages to
Cuba, but who will also save the cause of socialism for the rest
of the world and all posterity. Indeed, as when he confided in
his famous June 1958 letter that his "true destiny" was to wage
war against the United States, the struggle against resurgent
capitalism now serves as his new historic mission.

No one should take satisfaction from the conclusion the
Fidel will insist on being Fidel. The longer Cuba's inevitable
transition to a post-Castro polity and economy is delayed, the
more likely it will be that the Cuban people will suffer intense
violence and be ill-prepared to embark upon Cuba's reconstruction
through viable, democratic institutions. Such a violent-ridden,
unstable situation is precisely the one Cuban future most likely
to confront the United States with its greatest challenges.

CUBA IS MORE THAN A DOMESTIC POLITICAL ISSUE

Foreign policy generalists like to point out that Cuba
occupies an inordinate amount of importance in Congress and the
Executive Branch given the island's small size and lack of
economic and military might. The reason for this, according to
conventional wisdom, is that Cuba is primarily a domestic, not a
foreign policy issue. The Cuban-American community--especially
when the late Jorge Más Canosa was its spokesperson--exercises
undue influence over U.S. policy, because the electoral votes of
Florida and New Jersey weigh heavily in the calculations of both
political parties. Nevertheless, while recognizing the domestic
dimension of U.S.-Cuban policy, the Forum found that Cuba is a
foreign policy problem in its own right, affecting a number of
important U.S. national interests and concerns.

Immigration and the security of our borders is one such
interest. A new wave of uncontrolled migration from Cuba would
affect Florida adversely. It would require substantial U.S. air

and sea deployments to stem the tide of *balseros* (and smuggling operations), and carryout rescue operations in the Florida Straits. Cuba's potential for large-scale out migration stems from the acute economic crisis endured by the island's 11 million inhabitants for nearly a decade. The potential is made worse by the likelihood that Cubans will not recover their 1989 living standards for at least another decade if the economy's low or stagnant annual growth rates continue, as is expected to be the case.

Another critical interest for the United States concerns Cuba serving as a new offshore base for drug traffickers. Whether under the present or a successor government in Cuba, this scenario could well materialize if the economy does not recover and authority breaks down to the point the island becomes wide open to drug traffickers. Also, Cuba is unlike other Caribbean states because its Ministry of Interior has a cadre of well trained, internationally-connected intelligence personnel who could easily be used for government-sanctioned drug operations--or who could turn themselves into free-lance drug traffickers.

Additionally, Cuba retains its pivotal geostrategic importance by virtue of the fact that it commands vital sea-lanes of communication in the Caribbean. An unstable Cuba, whether under or after Castro, could also become a new, infectious source of instability in the region whether in the form of Cuban out migration to surrounding islands, or anti-government incursions into Cuba from Florida and nearby islands. In the worst of all scenarios, U.S. military intervention could be required to quell civil unrest on the island, should either the Castro government or its successor unravel.

The United States also has larger concerns regarding Cuba that transcend the island. Castro's Cuba remains the last redoubt of communism in the Western Hemisphere. His regime stands opposed to the most fundamental national interests underlying U.S. policy goals in Latin America in the post-Cold War era--the nurturing of civil society, the observance of basic human rights, the creation of viable democratic government, and the emergence of market-oriented economies. Hence, the United States cannot seek a "safe-landing" in Cuba by shoring up the regime there because what the United States does in Cuba--and what happens to the island--reflect and affect broader U.S. policy concerns in the hemisphere.

CONSTRAINTS ON U.S. POLICY OPTIONS

While the United States has clear interests at stake in Cuba today and after Castro, it has precious little maneuvering room in which to craft a policy that might more effectively promote those interests by inducing peaceful change in Cuba. Despite the view of some critics that Cuba policy could be easily changed, U.S. policy is hemmed in by several constraints that exist not only in the United States in the form of the exile community, but also--and perhaps more importantly--that arise from Castro and Cuba's political system. Both sets of constraints present major obstacles to more flexible, responsive policies toward Cuba.

As noted earlier, one problem facing U.S. policy makers is how to help the Cuban people without helping the Castro government. The Forum wrestled with this dilemma without coming up with a clear-cut solution. It could only propose in general that the United States should adopt new measures that would "reach around the Cuban government to the Cuban people." How to achieve this goal was subsequently, and more explicitly, outlined in the policy recommendations of the Task Force of the Council on Foreign Relations.

Another dilemma is how to justify to the Congress and the American public proactive policy initiatives that would promote greater people-to-people, information, and remittance flows into Cuba, without telegraphing their "subversive" intent to the Cuban government. Track II critics, for instance, claimed that the Cuban Democracy Act of 1992 gave the regime's hardliners needed ammunition to start cracking down on dissent in 1996, while curtailing contacts between intellectuals and researchers and their North American counterparts. They maintain that this reactive behavior by the regime is likely to be repeated with the new Administration measures.

Indeed, this came to pass on February 16, 1999, when the regime enacted a tough anti-crime, anti-subversive law. By imposing the death penalty and other heavy sanctions, the new law seeks to stamp out the upsurge in violent crimes and drug use that has accompanied increased foreign tourism on the island. But the law also employs loosely worded, catch-all provisions to repress dissidents and independent journalists who are judged to be collaborating with U.S. policy. It thus bans the introduction and dissemination of "subversive" materials in the country. It prohibits "collaboration" with foreign news media if such work furthers the U.S. embargo or related U.S. policy toward Cuba. And it establishes prison sentences of up to twenty years--as well as fines--for crimes that affect "the fundamental interests, political or economic," of the Cuban state. Hence, critics of current U.S. policy toward Cuba have a valid point in emphasizing that Washington should take into account the impact of its proactive policies on the allies of democracy and freedom within Cuba.

Surely, however, Castro and other hardliners don't need Track II-type language or objectives to see the pitfalls of a more open society for their communist regime. By holding U.S. policy responsible for the Castro government's behavior, moreover, many critics unintentionally excuse Cuban repression. In effect, they present U.S. policymakers with the Hobbesan's choice of doing nothing, thereby consigning the United States to accepting Cuba's present status quo, or lifting the embargo unilaterally and unconditionally on the presumption the new policy will help promote change.

Still another problem for the United States lies in Cuba's political system. As noted earlier, the state no longer is totalitarian because the island's economic crisis has sapped some of the state's ability to exercise the kind of all inclusive societal control that it once had. Nevertheless, Cuba remains in a post-totalitarian mode in which civil society has only recently begun to emerge, and pluralism is discouraged and actively repressed. Thus, apart from the Catholic Church and its affiliated relief agency, *Caritas*, only a few Protestant churches and other emerging civil society actors have been able to secure a modicum of autonomy from the state. This means that the United States has few genuine NGOs on the island that it can work with and nourish. Cuba's civil society will be constructed by Cubans. The United States role will be limited and insufficient.

In this respect, Cuba pretty much marches to its own drummer--or, more accurately, to Fidel Castro's drumbeat and that of his hardline followers--despite the country's nearly decade-long economic and political crises. This means that external actors are neither likely to be able to alter profoundly the government's economic and political policies, nor quicken the pace of reforms, as long as the Cuban leadership believes it is contrary to its interests to do so.

Hence, despite Cuba's dependence on investments and tourism from their respective countries, Spanish Prime Minister Felipe González, European Union Representative Manuel Marín, and Canadian Prime Minister Jean Chretien have all failed in wresting significant concessions from Castro with respect to opening up the economy and polity, and observing human rights. In early 1996, for example, Marín attempted to intercede personally with Castro by offering to broker a deal with the United States that would lead to accommodation between the two countries in exchange for the Cuban government's respect for the rights of *Concilio Cubano*, human rights activists, and dissidents. Instead, Marín's intervention prompted the Cuban leader's February 1996 crackdown on *Concilio Cubano* and other critics of his regime.[16]

---

[16]Regarding this incident, see Richard A. Nuccio, "It's Castro Who Keep His Country in Isolation," *Los Angeles Times*, January 16, 1998. Nuccio's account of Marin's mission was confirmed by the EU representative who addressed the Forum's first session in February.

This Cuban reality discourages the U.S. government from making conciliatory moves toward Cuba because, without a positive response from the Cuban side, such initiatives cannot long be sustained by the American body politic. The Carter Administration discovered this more than twenty years ago after it had been pursuing a conciliatory approach toward Havana. Just when there was much open talk in Washington and the press of further steps toward normalizing relations, Castro mounted his second armed intervention in Africa, this time in the Ogaden, in November 1977. His new incursion came scarcely two months after the opening of U.S. and Cuban Interests Sections, and it compelled the Administration to abandon its new policy line.

As the Forum noted, this same dynamic is certain to persist as long as Fidel Castro is on the scene if only because Cuba and the United States remain divided by contradictory interests: The U.S. goal of a more open, democratic and market-oriented Cuba is directly at odds with Castro's interests in maintaining himself in power, playing on the world stage, and assuring his defiant, anti-American legacy.

Irrespective of whether U.S. policy is conciliatory, confrontational, or a more subtle combination of carrots and sticks, this suggests that Castro will not dance save on his terms--at a minimum, the total abdication by the United States of its goal of a democratic Cuba, and the recognition of his government as it is presently constituted. Without an anticipated Cuban payoff, conciliatory initiatives toward Castro present the U.S. Government with a classic no-win situation.

THE QUESTION OF LIFTING THE EMBARGO

The making of U.S. Cuba policy is worsened by the Helms-Burton Law, signed in the panicked reaction to the Cuban shootdown, whereby President Clinton ceded much of his policy making authority on Cuba. Because the U.S. economic embargo is now locked into law, a majority of the 535 members of the House and

Senate must be mustered if this fundamental element of policy is to be changed.

As stated in the Summary of the Forum's May session, critics of current U.S. policy have a number of valid reasons for wanting to see Helms-Burton rescinded or at least softened:

- The sanctions prescribed by Helms-Burton against third-countries were intended to isolate Cuba, but they are increasingly isolating the United States.

- The embargo unfairly punishes the Cuban people and is seen as being unworthy of a great power.

- The law enables the Castro government to rally the Cuban people behind it and to blame the U.S. for the island's dire economic predicament.

- It prevents U.S. corporations from doing business in Cuba at a time when Canadian, Spanish, and other firms have invested more than $2 billion in the island.

- It further prevents most Americans from joining the nearly one and one-half million Canadian and European tourists who visited the island this year.

- The law's ban on business and tourism denies hard currency to the regime, but also precludes the kinds of people-to-people contact that could help shore-up Cuba's fledgling civil society and impel Cuba's eventual transition toward a more open society.

- In a crisis situation the law's attempt to limit Executive Branch authority over Cuba policy could lead to indecisiveness or undermine Congressional support for actions that are in the national interest.[17]

---

[17] In signing Helm-Burton, President Clinton simultaneously issued a legal opinion denying that his signature acceded to the law's clear intent to restrict the President's foreign policymaking authority. When announcing the January 1999 measures the Administration argued that under the Helms-Burton Law it retained the authority to change any *regulations* affecting Cuba policy. Several Members of Congress most responsible for the law's drafting challenged this interpretation of the law's affect on policy. This ambiguity is likely to remain unimportant until

Helms-Burton is thus bad public policy, particularly in the degree to which it intrudes on the foreign policymaking authority of the President, and because of its negative impact on our relations with allies.

Nevertheless, as several Forum participants maintained, the presumption that lifting the embargo at this time will help to open Cuba up, leading thereby to systemic change, is a dubious proposition: There is little evidence in Cuba or elsewhere to support the view that by lifting the embargo unilaterally and easing the island's economic plight, Cuba will begin a transition toward a more open society and polity   For decades, authoritarian governments in Latin America and Asia with relatively more open societies than Cuba, and significant economic and people-to-people contacts with the West, have withstood pressures for reform. Turning to Cuba itself, domestically popular policies of "constructive engagement" by Canada, Spain, France, Italy, and the European Union have protected their nationals' investments, but have done little to promote the cause of democracy and human rights on the island. Hence, "constructive engagement" has been no more effective in encouraging system change in Cuba than has the "failed" policy of the United States. Furthermore, the few liberalizing economic reforms that occurred in Cuba came when the island was in its deepest economic crisis, through the mid-1990s. Once the economic situation stabilized and began to improve, "irreversible" reforms slowed to a standstill, while the regime has clamped down on political dissent since the end of 1995.

Lifting the embargo also involves a question of timing if it is to have the desired, constructive effect. While the Castro regime has confounded many of its critics by surviving the collapse of the Soviet Union, the island's economic future remains

---

either circumstances require haste or the adoption of measures that are not popular with Congress. A violent, chaotic, and precipitous transition in Cuba would produce exactly these conditions.

collapse of the Soviet Union, the island's economic future remains grim and uncertain. Cuban authorities have now conceded that Gross Domestic Product grew at a rate of only one percent in 1998 --not the targeted 2.5 to 3.5 percent as had been planned--and the growth rate may have been lower still, according to independent economists. Given that another harvest shortfall is a virtual certainty in 1999, the overall outlook for the economy remains grim. Meanwhile, social tensions have not abated and could increase if there is another economic downturn.

Under these conditions, as many in the Forum pointed out, lifting the embargo could well serve as a powerful incentive for the regime *not* to enact deeper economic reforms. At least over the short- to medium-term, the embargo's unilateral lifting would effectively bail-out the Castro regime. It would strengthen Cuba's strong communist state, rather than weaken it as the embargo's critics contend, because much of the new infusion of American investment and tourist dollars would end-up in the coffers of the state. Additionally, European governments and banks would become more inclined to extend new lines of credit and lower interest loans to the Cuban government. With its economic prospects brightening, there would thus be less need for the regime to enact new reforms, with the result that the status quo most likely would continue to be perpetuated.

The issue of the embargo also goes beyond Cuba: lifting or maintaining the embargo could convey a very important signal to the rest of Latin America concerning the United States' commitment to democracy. In particular, the unconditional lifting of the embargo will give the impression that we are prepared to accommodate Fidel Castro, the hemisphere's last and longest remaining dictator. This will signal to other anti-democratic forces in the hemisphere--not only hardline military officers and oligarchs, but also President Fujimori in Peru, the PRI's "dinosaurs" in Mexico, and now President Chávez in Venezuela--that the promotion of liberal democracy, pluralism, and human rights is of lesser importance to Washington than are private American business interests, and that their anti-democratic measures are likely to escape punishment by the United States.

POSITIONING OURSELVES FOR A POST-CASTRO CUBA

If lifting the embargo would be unwise at this time, what policy steps are most sensible and prudent? Bearing in mind that each constructive policy recommendation has its limits and downside, here are some caveats and proposals:

1. The announced changes in U.S. policy in January 1999 are on the right track because, in seeking to strengthen civil society on the island, they are looking forward to a post-Castro future. The Administration should implement these measures promptly and move on to others recommended by the Council on Foreign Relations to promote the growth of civil society. However, the Cuban government's attempt to inhibit the growth of the building blocks of a vibrant civil society will continue to place strict limits on impact of these measures within Cuba.

Recommendations. As Forum participants cautioned, policy makers and Congress should not be too sanguine about Cuba's prospects for a peaceful democratic transition. Even as it seeks that goal, the United States needs to be prepared to deal with other, less desirable post-Castro outcomes, including a continuation of communist rule, military takeover, internal violence and upheaval, and/or a breakdown in government authority on the island.

2. Cuba is not Eastern Europe, the Soviet Union, or Nicaragua under the Sandinistas. It still has a relatively strong communist state, while civil society is weak and organized opposition is feeble and repressed. For these and other reasons, the Forum concluded, the present communist regime could well survive its founder's passing, with perhaps Raúl Castro, National Assembly President Ricardo Alarcón, and/or a senior army general like Sugar Minister General Ulíses Rosales Del Toro, sharing power. However, because of restrictions on diplomatic contact

between the United States and Cuba, there is little detailed understanding of what these men might mean for Cuba's future and relations with the United States.

Recommendations. Without restoring full diplomatic relations with Havana, the U.S. Government should remove petty obstacles to diplomatic contacts with members of the current government. In particular, it should expand existing contacts between Cuban and U.S. military, counternarcotics, and law enforcement officials at all levels. After all, the United States conducted periodic summits with its mortal enemy, the Soviet Union, during the Cold War.

3. Whatever its composition, any successor regime is certain to be weaker and less cohesive than when Fidel Castro was present. It would most likely see the rise once again of reformers within its ranks, as well as the retention of hardliners who were close to Fidel. As occurred in other communist successions, such a regime would probably be internally faction-ridden and without much popular support. It if is to survive and gain legitimacy, a post-Castro regime would need to embark on a new course that holds out the prospect of a rapid economic recovery for the Cuban people. It is precisely at this time that the United States will have its best opportunity to move any successor regime toward a more open polity and economy.

Recommendations. When this post-Castro moment occurs, the United States should use the embargo's lifting as leverage to induce the regime to commence the island's democratic transition. The prospect of conditionally lifting the embargo, moreover, could serve to strengthen the hand of reformist leaders within the successor regime. Additionally, the U.S. Government should be ready with a public diplomacy strategy, humanitarian aid program, and an economic and technical assistance program, to assure the Cuban people--and reformers within the new government--that the United States is prepared to respect the sovereignty and independence of a post-Castro Cuba, and to materially assist the island in its democratic transition.

4. Provided U.S. policy is not overtaken by events such as Castro's death or major unrest on the island, the idea of a National Bipartisan Commission on Cuba needs to be revisited after the presidential elections in the year 2,000. Were it do its work in an even-handed as well as bipartisan manner, without a predetermined policy outcome in mind, a Cuba commission could help find greater common ground between opposing sides of the Cuba issue, much as did The RAND Forum during its three sessions.

As was evident in the Forum, there is broad agreement within the policy community regarding the ultimate goal of U.S. policy—to promote a free, democratic, and market-oriented Cuba. The deeper, more intractable fault-lines concern the means by which to best achieve that objective. While this is certain to pose the thorniest issue for a Cuba commission, a stronger policy consensus nevertheless is sorely needed if the present tension between Congress and the Executive Branch over our Cuba policy is to be overcome.

Recommendations. The commission needs to propose replacing our present hodgepodge of policies with a more coherent strategy for dealing with Cuba as it is today, and with a Cuba that eventually will be without Castro. As noted above, once that historic moment occurs, the United States must be ready to help support Cuba's democratic transition, including by easing or conditionally lifting the embargo if it is still in place. The commission also needs to address the critical issue of future compensation for expropriated U.S. properties, and the more immediate issue of foreign investment in Cuba.

The United States has long sought to discourage such investments by other countries but without much success. Instead of continuing with such a policy, the commission might propose that the United States wage a world-wide campaign making foreign investment conditional on the Cuban government's respect for principles that promote worker and environmental rights, and that give all Cubans access to the products of such enterprises. The commission could then assess whether targeted openings in prohibitions on trade and investment by U.S. firms would advance the goal of a peaceful, democratic transition.

A future National Bipartisan Commission on Cuba would be both fitting and opportune. It would come some one hundred years after the island was freed from Spanish colonial rule following the Spanish-American War--and, lest we forget, the War of Independence fought by Cuban freedom fighters themselves over a three-year period, which was preceded by their Ten Years' War of 1868-1878. It would come after more than half a century of often strained relations between the United States and the semi-independent Republic of Cuba, during which Washington initially sent in troops to reoccupy the unstable island, and, then, thereafter made its presence felt through the U.S. Embassy, Wall Street, and such pro-American dictators as Geraldo Machado and Fulgencio Batista.

The commission would also come after four decades of dictatorship by Fidel Castro, who swiftly transformed his revolution into a communist one, aligned his government with the former Soviet Union, nearly ignited World War III, and, to this day, manipulates Cuban nationalism through his anti-American invective and defiance. More importantly, it would come when, sooner or later, Cuba will be without its socialist *caudillo*, thereby opening the way for the United States to end its interventionist impulses and help promote a genuine democratic transition on the island.

APPENDIX A
CUBA FORUM PARTICIPANTS[18]

I.   **Former U.S. Policymakers (Current Affiliation)**

A. Alberto Coll, Principal Deputy, Assistant Secretary of Defense
   (Strategy Department, U.S. Naval War College)
B. Paula Dobriansky, Deputy Assistant Secretary of State for Human
   Rights and Humanitarian Affairs (Washington Office, Council on
   Foreign Relations)
C. Luigi Einaudi, Ambassador to the OAS (Inter-American Dialogue)
D. Craig Fuller, Chief of Staff, President Bush (Kornferry Intnl.)
E. Mort Halperin, Senior Staff, NSC (20th Century Fund)
F. Stuart Lippe, Deputy Director, Office of Cuban Affairs, Dept. of
   State (World Bank)
G. Richard Nuccio, Senior Foreign Policy Advisor (Weatherhead Center
   for International Affairs, Harvard University); Forum Advisor
H. Peter Orr, Agency for International Development (Transition
   Specialist)
I. Phillip Peters, Director of Press and Public Affairs, Bureau of
   Inter-American Affairs, Department of State (Alexis de Tocqueville
   Institution)
J. Susan Kaufman Purcell, Policy Planning Staff, Department of State
   (Vice President, The Americas Society)
L. Michael Skol, Deputy Assistant Secretary of State (Skol and
   Associates, Inc.)
M. Gregory Treverton, Deputy Director, National Intelligence Council
   (International Security and Defense Policy Center, RAND)

II. **U.S. Senate and House of Representatives**

A. *Senators as Represented by Staff*

   1. Robert Filippone, Legislative Assistant for Bob Graham, FL (D)
   2. Joshua Shapiro, Advisor, Robert Torricelli, N.J. (D)
   3. Dan McGirt, Legislative Assistant for Paul Coverdell, GA (R)

---

[18]Not all participants attended all three sessions of the
Forum.

4. Randy Scheunemann, Advisor of Foreign Policy and Intelligence for Trent Lott, Miss (R)
5. Andy Semmel, Legislative Assistant for Richard G. Lugar, Ind. (R)
6. Gary Shiffman, Foreign Policy Advisor for Connie Mack, FL (R)
7. Mark Thiesen, Foreign Policy Advisor for Jesse Helms, NC (R)
8. Terrence Williams, Legislative Asst. for Sam Brownback, Ka. (R)

B. *Senate Committee Staff*

1. Foreign Relations Committee

    a) Roger Noriega, Professional Staff
    b) Janice O'Connell, Professional Staff
    c) Dawn Ratliff, Professional Staff

C. *Representatives as Represented by Staff*

1. Jodi Christiansen, Staff Assistant for Robert Menendez, NJ (D)
2. Charisse Glassman, Staff Assistant for Donald M. Payne, NJ (D)
3. Linda Luisi, Legislative Assistant for Howard Berman, CA (D)
4. Stephen Vermillion, Chief of Staff for Lincoln Diaz-Balart, FL (R)

D. *House of Representatives Committee Staff*

1. Committee on Intelligence
    a) Christopher Barton, Deputy Chief Counsel
    b) Merrill Moorhead, Professional Staff Member

2. Committee on International Relations
    a) Caleb McCarry, Professional Staff Member
    b) Denis McDonough, Professional Staff Member
    c) Yleem D.S. Poblete, Professional Staff Member

III. **Executive Branch and Other U.S.G. Representatives**

A. Jeffrey DeLaurentis, Director, Inter-American Affairs, National Security Council
B. James Dobbins, Special Assistant to the President and Senior Director for Inter-American Affairs, National Security Council
C. Myles Frechette, Ambassador, Department of State
D. Brig. Gen. John Goodman, USMC, U.S. Southern Command
E. Lt. Col. Emilio Gonzalez, U.S. Military Academy, West Point

F. Lt. Col. Rick Kilroy, Southern Command

G. Brian Latell, Director, Center for the Study of Intelligence

H. David E. Mutchler, Senior Advisor/Coordinator for Cuba, Agency for International Development

I. Lt. Com. Augustine Otero, U.S. Southern Command

J. Michael Ranneberger, Director, Office of Cuban Affairs, Department of State

K. Capt. Randy Robb, U.S. Southern Command

L. Lt. Commander Terrance Smith, U.S. Southern Command

M. Major Eric Stewart, U.S. Southern Command

N. Capt. Steve Wetzell, U.S. Southern Command

IV. Academic and Other Specialists

A. Gillian Gunn Clissold, Director, Caribbean Project, Georgetown University

B. Jorge I. Domínguez, Director, Weatherhead Center for International Affairs, Harvard University

C. Edward Gonzalez, Professor Emeritus, UCLA, Resident Consultant at RAND and Forum Organizer

D. Pedro José Greer, Jr., M.D., Assistant Dean, University of Miami School of Medicine

E. Peter Kornbluh, Senior Analyst, The National Security Archive, George Washington University

F. George Plinio Montalván, International Economist, Washington, D.C.

G. Michael Radu, Foreign Policy Research Institute

H. Jamie Suchlicki, Professor of History, University of Miami

I. Phyllis Greene Walker, Georgetown University, Forum Rapporteur

V. Foreign Guests (February 18)

A. Mark Entwhistle, Former Canadian Ambassador to Cuba

B. Hugo Paeman, Ambassador of the European Union in Washington, D.C.

VI. Catholic Church Spokesperson (May 28)

A. Bishop William Murphy, Archdiocese of Boston

VII. General Policy Research NGO Spokespersons (May 28)

A. C. Richard Nelson, Director, International Security Program, Atlantic Council
B. Kimberly Healey, Senior Fellow, National Policy Association (Observer)
C. Kathleen M. Donahue, Center for International Policy

VIII. Cuba-Specific NGO Spokespersons (May 28)

A. Frank Calzon, Executive Director, Center for a Free Cuba
B. José R. Cárdenas, Washington Director, Cuban-American National Foundation
C. Craig Fuller (Kate Donohue, Lisa Weinmann after Fuller speaks), Americans for Humanitarian Trade with Cuba
D. Marifeli Pérez-Stable, Cuban Committee for Democracy

IX. The Ford Foundation

A. Cristina Eguizábal

APPENDIX B: DISCUSSION TOPICS FOR THE THREE SESSIONS
Discussion Topics for February 19-20 Forum Session

Although several of the following questions cannot be answered definitively, precisely or with brevity, their purpose is to stimulate thinking about what has been going on in Cuba as well as provide a topical agenda for the discussion periods. Some questions may not be explicitly raised by the Moderator or will be combined because of overlap or because of the way the discussion is flowing. Still other issues not mentioned below are certain to be raised by forum participants. The questions have been arranged at the system, elite, societal, and individual levels of analysis.

Discussion Topics at the System Level

1. Cuba has undergone economic, political and societal changes since the collapse of the Soviet Union in 1991. How does Cuba today differ from the Cuba of a decade ago? Has "system change" occurred?

2. Defying initial predictions and expectations, the Castro government remains in power seven years after the disappearance of the Soviet Union. What accounts for the regime's staying power?

3. Is Cuba's transition from a totalitarian communist state *sui generis*? Or are there similarities to other transitions that took place in the former Soviet Union, Eastern bloc countries, China, and Vietnam? Are there any similarities to non-communist transitions, such as Franco's Spain or Pinochet's Chile?

4. Cuba's economic crisis appears to have stabilized despite poor harvests over the past two years. How has the government arrested the economy's free fall? Are foreign investments, tourism, and other measures taken by the government sufficient to sustain an economic rebound or can we expect economic stagnation or downturn in the future?

5. What are the major forces driving Cuba's limited reforms? Are they elite and/or societal driven? Are Fidel and the hardliners in the regime the sole impediments to deeper reforms?

6. Will an improvement in the overall economy impel the regime toward more economic reforms and political liberalization? Or, conversely, is an upturn in the economy just as likely to produce the opposite result?

Discussion Topics at the Elite Level Inside the Regime

1. Who is Fidel Castro? Is he force for or obstacle to change? Is he concerned with the legacy he will leave for Cuba when he departs? If so, what steps is he taking to ensure his legacy? Or is he concerned only with his power, international status, and place in history?

2. Who is Raúl Castro? As Fidel's designated successor, will he pursue policies similar to those of his brother, or will he take a different

route, especially on economic policy? Will he be capable of making fundamental changes if he wants to?

3. Who are the "hardliners"? What do they stand for? Are they solely dependent upon Fidel? Or do they have sources of institutional and/or popular support?

4. What does the political profile of the second-tier leaders--Ricardo Alarcon, Carlos Lage, Roberto Robaina, et. al., look like? Do their views differ at all from those of Fidel? Is there a Gorbachev or Deng Xiao Ping among them?

5. Are the new generation of younger Party and government leaders committed "Leninists" who are driven by considerations of power and ideology? Or are they prospective "reformed communists" who want a more open economy and polity for Cuba if not now, after Castro?

6. How has the fall of communism affected mid- and lower-level Party cadres and government functionaries? Have they embraced Cuba's limited reforms, including the dollarization of the economy, and the Pope's visit? Or are they a recalcitrant, conservative force?

7. The FAR is widely considered Cuba's strongest institution, one that is likely to play a determining role in a post-Castro Cuba. Is the military a conservative status quo force, valuing its own institutional interests, and national sovereignty and order above all else? Or is it a potential force for system-change--one that could favor a more market-oriented economy and a more open polity?

8. In the event of civil strife that cannot be controlled by the Ministry of Interior, would FAR units fire on civilians?

9. If a succession crisis overtakes the regime, and/or social tensions intensify greatly because of a worsening economy, would the FAR generals and colonels favor a military takeover?

Discussion Topics at the Elite Level Outside the Regime

1. The Catholic Church is widely considered Cuba's strongest institution outside the state, one that has been re-energized by the Pope's visit. What role does the Church see itself playing in Cuba's current transition process? What role does Fidel see it playing?

2. Is the Catholic Church's influence limited by Cuban population's lack of Catholic religiosity and attraction to Santería? How influential can the essentially all white Catholic priesthood be in a society that is more than 50 percent black and mulatto?

2. Intellectuals have played critical precursor roles in fomenting revolutionary change not only historically in Cuba, but also in the Soviet Union and Eastern Europe. Does the precursor role apply to

Cuba's intelligentsia in Cuba today? Do they have a potential role in accelerating change?

3. Apart from Catholic and Santería priests, are there political dissidents, human rights activists, evangelical pastors, trade unionists, small entrepreneurs, etc.., who are capable of attracting a mass following as a counter-elite? Or are they unlikely to ever present much of a challenge to the regime?

Discussion Topics at the Societal Level

1. How is Cuba's *líder máximo* viewed by his people? Is he still the charismatic "Fidel," capable of moving the masses and doing no wrong? Has he become "Castro," the *caudillo* interested only in preserving his power no matter the costs to Cuban society? Or is he now "*el loco*" or "*el viejo*" to many Cubans who wish he would pass away?

2. How is the "revolution" perceived by most Cubans? As a revolution that has bestowed national sovereignty and dignity, greater equality and national pride, and a host of social goods for the majority of Cubans? Or as a failed revolution that has created economic misery, new class divisions, new social inequities, and a hopeless future?

3. How is the "regime" perceived by the average Cuban? As a government that is concerned with the overall welfare of the people? Or as one that is generally impervious to the people's suffering?

4. How do Cuban youths differ in their political views and values from older generations? Are they a source of regime support, an apathetic, apolitical sector of the population, or an emerging source of regime opposition?

5. What do the Cuban people want and expect from government? Would they prefer a benign authoritarian socialist-type government that maintains order, controls the economy, and redistributes social goods? Or would they favor a more liberal democratic government that relies largely on the workings of the free market for economic growth and development?

6. What is the reaction of the average Cuban to the influx of foreign investments and tourists? Is there a nationalist reaction developing toward the privileges enjoyed by foreigners? Toward the resurgence of prostitution and sex tourism? Toward the reintroduction of a dollar economy? Has regime legitimacy eroded because of these developments?

7. Outside the Catholic Church, are there signs that a civil society is emerging in Cuba? Is there any evidence that civil society actors-- independent political groups, private sector associations, labor unions, religious organizations, self-help groups, etc.--are becoming strong enough to bargain with the state for more political, economic, and cultural space?

8. If fundamental change eventually comes to Cuba, will civil society play a role in impelling such change from below as was the case in some

of the East European states and, to a lesser degree, in the Soviet Union? Or will change come from the top, from within the regime itself, because of the absence of a civil society?

9. What is the perception of the average Cuban toward the exile community in Miami? Is it seen as a threat? A source of life-saving remittances? A future haven? A constructive or destructive force in a new Cuba?

10. Is Santería a religion and societal force that favors the status quo and the regime? What of the Protestant and evangelical churches?

11. Save for the disturbances on the Havana waterfront in 1994, why has the Cuban population been so accepting of its fate? Why have dissidents not been able to galvanize a broader popular following? Are the regime's totalitarian-type control mechanisms the reason? Or are there other factors and dynamics at work?

12. If popular opposition to the regime were to manifest itself, how would it start? In the form of organized resistance directed by opposition movements led by dissidents and political leaders? Or in the form of spontaneous combustion--anomic rioting and other unstructured forms of civil disorder?

13. Were civil strife to break out in Cuba, where would it most likely occur? In urban or rural areas? In Havana or other cities? In eastern, central, or western Cuba?

Discussion Topics at the Individual Level

1. After nearly four decades of living under a revolutionary or communist regime, have Cubans undergone a change in their personal values, norms and expectations? Do they differ all that much from Cuban exiles in Florida and elsewhere?

2. How have Cubans responded to the increased hardships--from shortages of foodstuffs, basic necessities, and medicines, to electricity, public transportation and fuel--associated with the "Special Period"? What are their mechanisms of daily survival?

3. Do Cubans blame Fidel and/or the government for their plight?

4. What are the social safety-valves that enable Cubans to endure or escape conditions of extreme privation if not hopelessness? Is it religion? Prostitution? Corruption? Migration? Other?

5. How do Cubans feel about teenagers and young women becoming *jineteras*, going out with or having sex with foreign tourists, and in some instances marrying foreigners? How does all this impact on the traditional Cuban family? On relationships and marriages?

6. Given the reported modest improvement in the economy, do Cubans have rising expectations that their life will get better? Do they have hope for their children's future?

7. Are *Habaneros* better off than the majority of their countrymen? Or are Cubans who reside elsewhere in the countryside or in other towns and cities better able to survive food and other shortages?

Questions to Ponder Concerning Where Cuba is Headed

1. What will Cuba look like five years hence? An extension of present-day Cuba? A democratic Cuba with a market-oriented economy? Other...?

2. What are the prospects over the next five years or so for:

- Prolonged regime decay during which little change takes place?

- Successful regime-managed system change along peaceful, evolutionary lines?

- Eventual system breakdown followed by military takeover?

- Violent system change as a result of leadership instability at the top and/or uncontrolled societal pressures from below?

- Peaceful change and national reconciliation through a new government that includes present regime leaders and their political opponents?

- Other...?

Discussion Topics for the April 16-17 Session of The RAND Forum on Cuba

As with the first session of the RAND Forum on Cuba, the following questions are intended to stimulate thinking about what are U.S. interests in Cuba, including the U.S. stakes in different transition outcomes. The questions are to serve as a general agenda guide for the April 16th session, in which the Moderator may raise, reformulate, and/or combine some of the questions in order to promote discussion among participants. Several questions are relevant to the briefing to be presented in the afternoon. As readily seen, some of the questions overlap.

Discussion Topics at the General Level

1. What have been the "old" or traditional strategic, economic, and political interests that the United States has historically pursued in Cuba? In what way has Castro's Cuba affected these interests in the past? Are they being similarly endangered today?

2. How are "new" U.S. interests and concerns over human rights, democracy, illicit drug flows, and illegal immigration, affected by today's Cuba? Is Cuba any worse of a problem or offender with respect to these new interests and concerns than, let's say, Mexico, Guatemala, or Colombia?

3. Now that the Cold War is over, why should Castro's Cuba matter in a post-communist world? How can an island of 11 million people, mired in an economic crisis, and no longer aligned with a hostile world power, adversely U.S. interests, new or old? Does Guantanamo Naval Base still possess much military utility?

4. Why should the United States be concerned about the kind of political and economic system that Cuba has when the order of battle for Cuba's Revolutionary Armed Forces has been so degraded that the FAR no longer possesses much of a military capability? Or does Cuba today still present a credible military threat to its Caribbean neighbors and the United States?

5. Is the outcome of Cuba's present transition process of "vital interest" to the United States? If not, can the fate of the island nonetheless potentially affect the "national interest" of the United States?

6. Is Cuba's importance to U.S. interests, new and old, of such a magnitude that the United States should be prepared to risk damaging relations with its European and Latin American allies?

7. In addition to being conflictive, are the interests of the Castro leadership also in fundamental contradiction to those of the United States that involve the promotion of democracy, human rights, and a market economy?

64

Discussion Topics Concerning Cuba Today

1. Does the FAR retain any offensive capability to speak of? What would be most likely conflict scenario in which the Cuban armed forces would be deployed? Civil disorder? Exile over flights or incursions? An unprovoked attack on Guantanamo? An attack against south Florida in a war engineered by Castro? As "internationalist volunteers" to aid Marxist rebels abroad? Other?

2. To what extent, if any, does Cuba today still engage in the promotion of revolution abroad and the subversion of other hemispheric states? If it does, what revolutionary groups does it cultivate and support? What Latin governments are its targets?

3. Assuming Fidel Castro's continued hostility to the United States, in what way can he endanger "old" or "new" U.S. interests? Put another way, is there a significant disconnect between Castro's "intentions" and Cuba's present military or subversive "capabilities" with respect to the United States or other Caribbean or Latin American states?

4. Now or in the near-term future, should we be concerned that Cuba may present a threat of biological warfare for the United States and the Caribbean because of its bio-medical industry? Or is this but a remote possibility?

5. Although Cuba does not possess a nuclear arsenal, should we be worried that the island's $1.2 billion nuclear plant facility near Juragua could go on-line if the Castro government secures sufficient additional funding to finish the plant? Should this concern be over the possible military usage of nuclear material from the plant, or the plant's potential for suffering a catastrophic failure like Chernobyl?

6. To what extent, if any, has Cuba become a base for illicit drug flows to the United States? If it is involved in drug trafficking, is this a conscious policy of the Castro government or the result of free-lancing by corrupt individuals operating under a weakened, decaying state?

7. Has the Cuban government developed links to Latin American or other drug cartels? If so, what institutions or organizations within the regime are principally responsible for such linkages?

8 Is the Lourdes electronic facility still actively used as a listening post for intercepting U.S. government and private communications? Does it present a major problem for the U.S. military? For U.S. corporations? For U.S. scientific and academic institutions?

9. What are the most likely circumstances in which there would occur uncontrolled migration from Cuba? As a conscious policy decision by the Castro government? As a result of a renewed economic downturn? As a result of heightened government repression and civil disorder?

10. In the worst of circumstances, what would be the magnitude of uncontrolled migration from Cuba? Would the outflow take the form of Mariel or the 1994 migration crisis? Would it be aimed at Guantanamo? Could the Castro government reassert control? Could the United States prevent or stem the outflow?

Discussion Topics for a Cuba After Fidel Castro

1. What outcome for a post-Castro Cuba would be worst for U.S. interests? A new Cuba wracked by prolonged civil unrest or war from which there may or may not emerge a new government committed to democracy and a free market? A new Cuba that remains stable under a "new team" headed by Raúl Castro and Ricardo Alarcón? A new Cuba in which order is preserved under a military government? A new Cuba in which the elected government is scarcely able to govern, is corrupt, and is increasingly penetrated by drug traffickers?

2. Were Raúl Castro, Ricardo Alarcón, and other members of the present regime to constitute a new successor government and seek normal relations with the United States, what interests and concerns should the U.S. Government insist be respected? Were the new government to be confirmed in power by internationally supervised elections, should it be recognized?

3. Were Cuba to be plunged into civil war following Fidel Castro's death or incapacitation, under what conditions should the United States consider armed intervention? To prevent Raúl Castro and other communist leaders from winning the conflict? To end the bloodletting, restore order, and/or prevent further human rights abuses? To stem the tide of illegal immigration from the island? To end the killing of present members of the regime by a vengeful population and successor government? To prevent elements connected to drug traffickers from taking over the island? To install a new government committed to democracy?

4. Once Fidel Castro has departed the scene, will the United States and the "new Cuba" enter a new period of reconciliation and harmony? Or are there likely to be enduring conflicts of national interest between the two countries that will linger on and remain divisive to the relationship? In other words, are there permanent divisive interests that transcend whatever U.S. administration is in office and whatever Cuban government succeeds the present Cuban regime?

5. What historic pattern of relationship between the United States and Cuba would most probably reassert itself after Castro is gone? The re-imposition of U.S. hegemony over the island (1898-1933)? The dawning of a new era of harmony and mutual respect (1933-45)? The return to a new policy of neglect (1946-59)?

Discussion Topics for the May 28-29 Session of
The RAND Forum on Cuba

The following questions are intended to stimulate thinking on current and future U.S. policy toward Cuba, which is the topic for the final Forum session in May. They build on the deliberations of the February and April Forum sessions, particularly the general conclusions reached in those discussions. Many explore the intrinsic ambiguities and hard choices that need to be made in U.S. policy toward a Cuba under and after Castro.

Discussion Topics at the General Level

1. Given the Forum's conclusions concerning Castro's intransigence toward system change, and the irreconcilability of his core interests with ours, should U.S. policy continue trying to promote "peaceful change" in today's Cuba? Or should we strive for fundamental change irrespective whether of it comes about by peaceful or violent means?

2. Given the broad spectrum of interests and moral concerns that the Forum identified with respect to Cuba, what policy trade-offs are acceptable to the United States? The promotion of U.S. economic interests and business opportunities at the cost of democracy and human rights? A "safe-landing" in Cuba and a "drug-free" island irrespective of whether they are realized under an authoritarian or democratic government? A more open but possibly unstable or crime-ridden Cuba?

3. Does the fact that the regime has survived the 36 year-old U.S. embargo while also resisting change in itself constitute sufficient grounds for jettisoning the embargo? Or are there other criteria for measuring the embargo's success or failure?

4. How much of an obstacle does the claims issue present in normalizing relations with Cuba? Is it likely to be worked out at the beginning or the end of negotiations? What compensation formula might be expected?

5. From a moral standpoint, how can the U.S. justify an embargo that punishes the Cuban people more than the regime? Conversely, can lifting the embargo be morally justified if it would enable the regime to perpetuate itself even were the lot of the Cuban people to be improved?

6. From a moral as well as practical policy standpoint, should the United States pursue reconciliation with a dictatorship if there is little likelihood of fundamental change in the years ahead?

7. Should U.S. Cuba policy assume that the United States would have to deal with future developments in Cuba unilaterally and, therefore, not preoccupy itself with coordinating policy with others? Or, is it likely that the United States will need multilateral support for its post-Castro efforts? What concessions, if any, should U.S. policy make to other governments to attract their support?

Policy Questions Regarding Helms-Burton

1. With respect to promoting fundamental change in Cuba, have the sanctions codified under the Helms-Burton Law been effective in their objectives? Where and why have they failed? What changes in the law would make it a more effective policy instrument?

2. From the perspective of the Executive Branch, what problems and advantages does Helms-Burton present for our Cuba policy? What are the problems and advantages from the perspective of Congress? Is there a fundamental divide between Congress and the Executive Branch over Cuba?

3. Has Congressional as well as White House support for Helms-Burton eroded to the extent that the law might be rescinded? What factors work in favor of the law remaining in force? What factors work against it?

4. Assuming that it has had the effect of denying or discouraging some foreign investments in Cuba, has Helms-Burton been worth the friction that it has created between the U.S. and the European Union, Canada, and other allies?

5. What are the reasons why the additional protection of Helms-Burton was seen as necessary beyond the registered claims procedures already in place for owners of expropriated property? What should be the place of concerns about expropriated in overall U.S. policy? Is there a potential conflict between placing a priority settlement and the governability of a post-Castro transitional regime?

6. What can be done under Helms-Burton to better nurture civil society in Cuba and weaken regime cohesion? Or does Helms-Burton work at cross purposes with such policy objectives?

Policy Questions Regarding Alternatives to Helms-Burton

1. In terms of its moral standing and policy objectives, what would U.S. lose in Cuba, the Caribbean and Latin America, and the broader international community, were Washington to lift the embargo? What would be the expected gains?

2. What would happen inside Cuba if the embargo were lifted with or without conditions? Would the regime be strengthened or weakened? What would be Castro's reaction? The reaction of the Cuban people?

3. What evidence is there that a "policy of engagement" is more likely to produce change toward a more open economy and polity under Castro than has been the case with our current policy? Have the Spanish, Canadian, and Latin American governments, or the European Union, been successful in gaining political and human rights concessions from the Castro government? Has engagement succeeded in liberalizing or

undermining other authoritarian regimes like those of China, Singapore, or Chile under Pinochet?

4. Given that Cuba under Castro remains a contentious issue in U.S. domestic politics, can a policy of engagement be sustained if it does not produce political and economic liberalization in Cuba? If the Castro regime not only rejects change but intensifies its repression and controls in Cuba, and its attacks on Washington?

5. If a policy of engagement were not to lead to fundamental change in Cuba, are there still other gains that could be achieved through such a policy? Would these be sufficient to offset the lack of change by the regime?

6. Are there ways that the United States can help the Cuban people without helping to perpetuate the Castro regime or its succession by a similar dictatorship?